English, Indiana

English, Indiana
Memories of Main Street

BY

E. C. Roberts

AS TOLD TO NICK ROBERTS

Indiana University Press

BLOOMINGTON AND INDIANAPOLIS

The paper used in this publication meets the minimum requirements of American National Standard for Information Sciences—Permanence of Paper for Printed Library Materials, ANSI Z39.48-1984.

MANUFACTURED IN THE UNITED STATES OF AMERICA

Library of Congress Cataloging-in-Publication Data

Roberts, E. C.
English, Indiana : memories of Main Street / by E. C. Roberts as told to Nick Roberts.
p. cm.
ISBN 0-253-35032-8 (cloth)
1. English (Ind.)—Social life and customs. 2. Roberts, E. C. I. Roberts, Nick. II. Title.
F534.E59R63 1991
977.2'28—dc20 91-6301

1 2 3 4 5 95 94 93 92 91

For Dad

CONTENTS

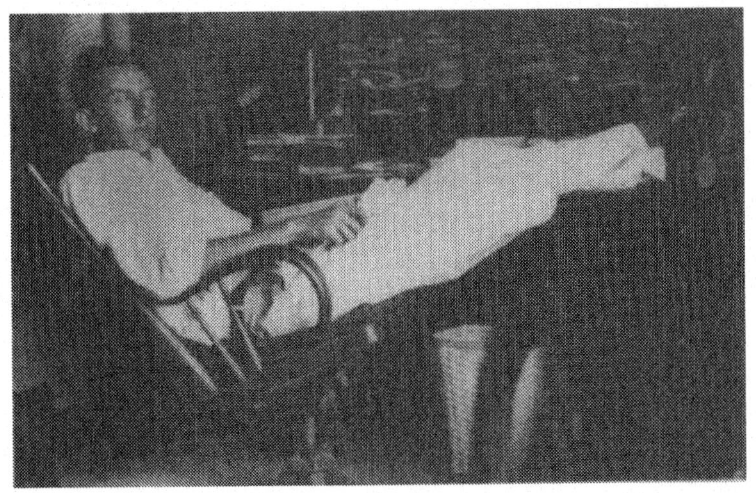

E. C. Roberts (about 1929)

Acknowledgments

The original reason for this manuscript was to help celebrate the sesquicentennial of my hometown. A few stories and remembrances would be typed up, maybe published in the local paper, and copies would be circulated to family and friends, with a copy or two filed at the public library.

Somewhere along the way, Jeanna Michaels suggested that the stories might be interesting enough to entertain even those—like herself—who knew only that Indiana was somewhere west of Pittsburgh and East of Las Vegas. John Gallman at the Indiana University Press agreed, and suddenly I was an author.

Jewell Sears, at the Crawford County Public Library, and Sara Combs and Karen Byerly, at the offices of the *Crawford County Democrat,* made their files of newspapers available to verify dates and events. The ads and articles reproduced in this book would not have been available without their help.

Thelma Sloan kindly made her extensive—and fascinating—family records available. Curtis and Carol Benham, Joe Levine, and Anne Howard Bailey gave much-appreciated assistance and support whenever asked.

And, to all those who lived the stories that follow, thanks for giving me something worthy of remembering.

English, Indiana

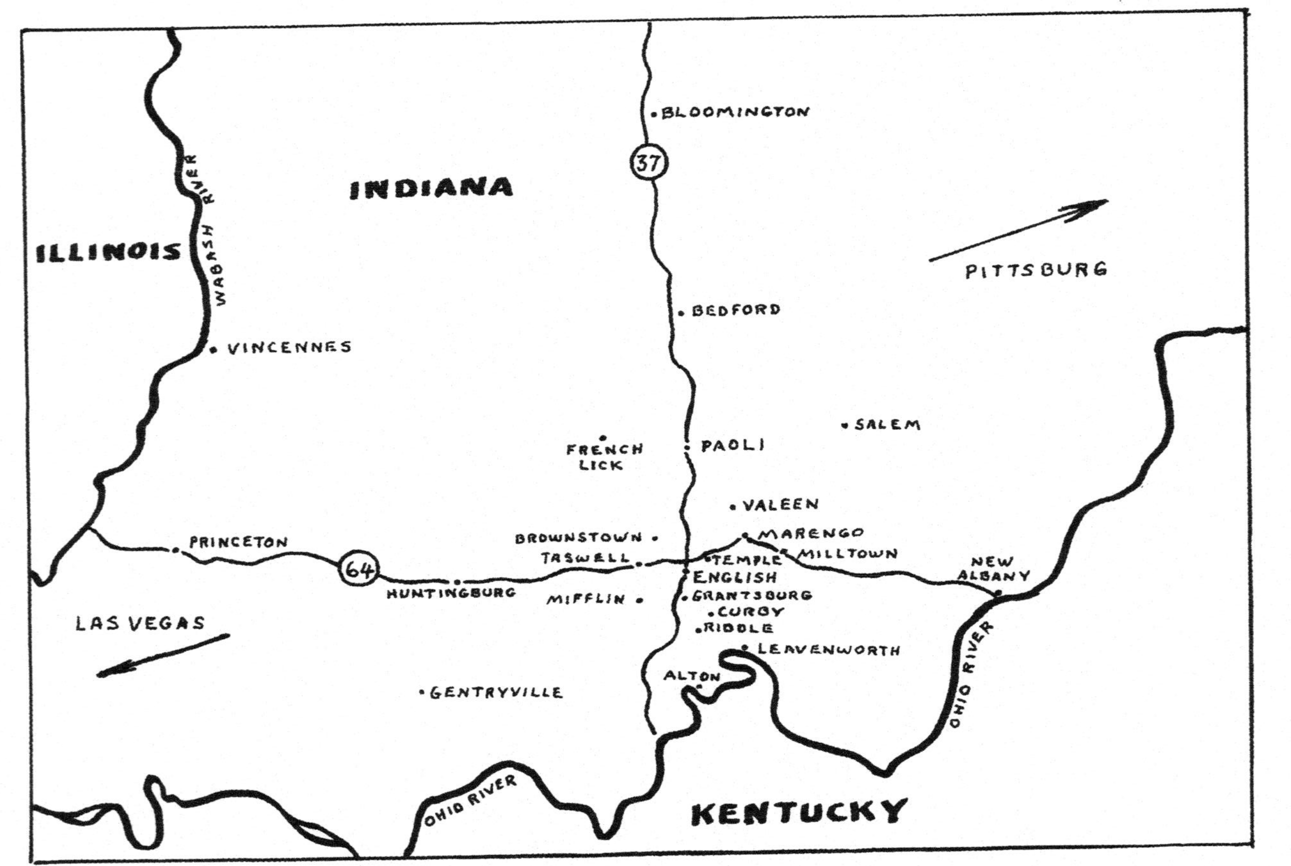

ILLINOIS
INDIANA
WABASH RIVER
BLOOMINGTON
37
PITTSBURG
BEDFORD
VINCENNES
SALEM
FRENCH LICK
PAOLI
VALEEN
PRINCETON
BROWNSTOWN
MARENGO
TASWELL
TEMPLE
MILLTOWN
64
ENGLISH
NEW ALBANY
HUNTINGBURG
MIFFLIN
GRANTSBURG
CURBY
RIDDLE
LAS VEGAS
LEAVENWORTH
ALTON
GENTRYVILLE
OHIO RIVER
OHIO RIVER
KENTUCKY

Motivation

Thomas Lincoln was a typical victim. Three times he had acquired land in Kentucky and three times there had been a faulty deed or an error in the survey or something that meant the land wasn't his after all. Enough was enough. Thomas packed up his family and few belongings and moved to a new Promised Land, a fertile, forested territory to the north where land titles were safe: Indiana.

The Lincoln family found a home near Gentryville, an already thriving community. Other settlers opted to carve out their own niches farther up in the wilderness, which must have seemed as limitless as the sky above. Indiana welcomed them all, and they welcomed the opportunity.

Except that Thomas's son, young Abe, made a name for himself later on, the Lincoln family would have disappeared into the early pages of Indiana history. Thousands of others had no presidents in their progenies, but their stories must be no less compelling. They, too, wanted something better in their lives and came to Indiana to find it. By choice or chance, they became neighbors and built communities from the native logs. Eventually, they coined names for each cluster of cabins and connecting trails. Until then, most settlements were known to the inhabitants by a simple, shared name: Home.

What follows is about one of those settlements. The one I still call Home.

Over the River and Through the Woods

Highway 64 crosses over State Road 37 right at the north edge of English, Indiana, making a convenient X to mark the location of a significant, historic site—significant, at least, to this book.

In June of 1814, James G. Sloan left his home in Barren County, Kentucky, and crossed the Ohio River to New Albany, on the edge of the Indiana Territory. James was anxious to take advantage of the law allowing settlers to buy land in the new territory at two dollars per acre, paying a fourth down and the balance in four annual installments.

A neighbor from Barren County, Joseph Kinkaid, had preceded him in March, electing to brave the remnants of winter so he could file for some land, build his cabin, and be ready for spring planting. In order to leave Kentucky before his farm was sold, Kinkaid had entrusted James's father, Archibald, with his power of attorney. Now that everything was finalized, James was on his way with Kinkaid's profits from the sale and enough money to make a down payment on some land of his own.

James hiked west for about fifty miles, following Kinkaid's instructions as to which ridges and hollows and streams to use as landmarks. Hostilities with the Indians had only ceased the previous September, and when James, who was carrying only a muzzleloading rifle and an axe, came across three young braves cooking meat over a fire, he had no way of knowing if they would be friendly. He backtracked, continued south through another valley, and eventually located Joseph Kinkaid's new home, situated on one hundred sixty acres of rich bottom land that included a small stream.

He learned that Kinkaid's nearest neighbor was a man named Moses Smith, who owned eighty acres about a half mile south, where the stream joined a creek flowing east to west. Sloan found a good spring immediately south of Kinkaid's property, made the three-day trek to the land office at Vincennes, filed for the adjacent eighty acres (forty dollars down with four yearly payments of thirty dollars), walked back to his new home, and started work on a cabin. When he discovered a better spring in a nearby hill, he built another cabin and moved from the northwest to the southeast quadrants of the X that would be made by the two highways 150 years later.

This move put him within the present-day city limits, fronting what would someday become a major thoroughfare. And, since State Road 37 is the only north/south route through English, it's known by another name between the city limits. James Sloan never knew it, but he had become the first homeowner on Main Street.

* * *

One day, in about 1950, I was talking with Arch Sloan on the front porch of the two-story frame house that had eventually enveloped his grandfather's second cabin. Arch pointed to the rise where the original cabin had been and told me that the foundation of that first cabin had only recently been removed by the present owner of the land.

About 1980, after Arch and his sister, Blanche, had passed away, a fire damaged the house and everything but the log cabin built by James Sloan was removed. By standing back and looking from the right place, you could almost imagine that it was 1818, Indiana was a brand-new state, and James Sloan was somewhere nearby in his fields, working to pay the last annual installment that would make the land his, free and clear.

In 1985, the logs were bought by a real estate company in Bedford and were taken away to be reconstructed as part of a pioneer village.

James Sloan's Cabin (1985)

THE EARLY SETTLER

Sometimes it's mighty peaceful
In our cabin here at night,
When all the kids are in their beds
And everything gets quiet.

We roll a backlog on the fire
Then settle down for good,
By the flick'ring from the fireplace
And the cracklin' of the wood.

A moonbeam through the window
Casts a pale and eerie light,
And the sounds deep in the forest
Break the stillness of the night.

It's easy to feel lonely
And remember all life's ills,
Yet we always feel God's presence
In these Crawford County Hills.
E. C. Roberts

Hartford

The stream that flowed through Joseph Kinkaid's property and past James Sloan's cabin was one of three that came together on Moses Smith's property, a half mile to the south, forming Little Blue River. Smith was willing to sell individual pieces of his bottom land and a few newcomers bought whatever they could and built cabins. The resulting settlement became known, logically enough, as Three Forks of Little Blue.

For twenty-five years, not much changed. In 1839, Wilson Scott made a plat of the town he called "Hartford" and recorded it on April 9th at Fredonia. Scott's plat showed streets and lots neatly laid out to the east and north of the existing settlement. Main Street finally existed—on paper. In 1840, Bry Gregory was granted a license to run a saloon, and two years later Joseph Denbo opened a store. Hartford was now officially a town with all the necessary ingredients for growth—except one: You couldn't get there from anywhere.

Wilson Scott was one of Indiana's first serious real estate developers and, like many visionaries, he was also a few decades ahead of his time. Not surprisingly, all the people who couldn't get to Hartford didn't show up.

Twenty years later, on the eve of the Civil War, W. W. Cum-

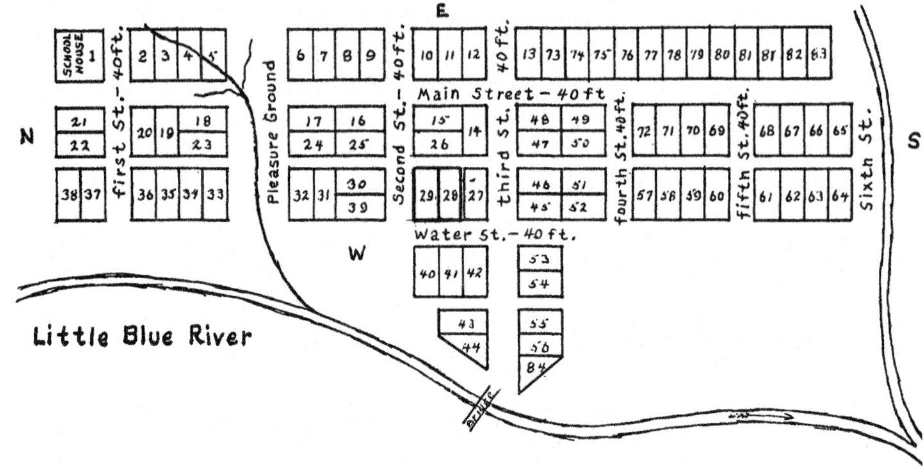

Wilson Scott Plat (1839) | Cummins Addition (1860)

mins bought up Scott's property and added it to his own, located just south of the Hartford plat. He filed a new plat and the size of the town doubled—on paper.

The most interesting thing about the Cummins Addition is that it shows where the town *wasn't*. The blank spot on the lower right is where all the homes and businesses were located—about a dozen cabins and a couple of stores. Like Wilson Scott, W. W. Cummins was also ahead of his time. In spite of all the plats and plans, new residents still stayed away in droves.

Finally, in the early 1880s the Air Line came through Hartford and you *could* get there from anywhere. (The Air Line Railroad, that is, later to become the Southern.) My father-in-law, William A. Young, told me that he and John Will Megenity quit their jobs working on a farm near Valeen and walked to Hartford to hire in on the new railroad. The pay was a dollar a day, plus room and board. The railway had a barracks and a cookhouse about a mile west of town. Bill drove a mule with a dumpcart hauling rock and dirt to make the fill for the Tory Miller trestle.

The hilly southern Indiana topography dictated that the railroad come through at the south edge of town. The best place to put the depot turned out to be not in the existing business district, but at the end of . . . Main Street. Since building a railroad meant lots of hungry, thirsty workers, saloons and other businesses began to appear. The future—and Main Street—had arrived with the locomotive.

And the past was about to be swept clean.

The election of 1880 was memorable for the citizens of Hartford in that their former congressman, William H. English, was the running mate of Winfield S. Hancock, the Democratic presidential candidate. By a margin of one-tenth of one percent in the popular vote, the Hancock/English ticket lost to the Garfield/McKinley ticket.

The citizens of Hartford were, however, sufficiently impressed by their former congressman's notoriety to change the name of their town. In 1884, "Hartford" joined "Three Forks of Little Blue" in the history books. The community would be known to the approaching new century as English, Indiana.

Captain Jack

Prior to the coming of the railroad, commerce depended on the rivers. Leavenworth, on the Ohio, had become the predominant town in Crawford County after the Civil War, and, not surprisingly, was the county seat. Now, however, English had the railroad and a convenient central location. Clearly, the future pointed to a county seat at English.

In 1893, a special meeting was held and a committee was formed. Petitioners were appointed to canvas the county. Sixty-five percent of the voters agreed that English should be the new county seat. The results were presented to the county commissioners, who ordered that the courthouse be moved. The people had spoken and their voice had been heard.

Well . . . almost.

The people of Leavenworth kind of liked having the county seat in their town, so they took the case to court. The trial lasted about three weeks, and English won. A new courthouse was planned and over two acres of land was donated on a hill at the south edge of town. The future was once again secure.

Well . . . not quite.

The people of Leavenworth, not being very good losers, got two judges to issue an injunction, which stopped everything. A special judge was appointed to hear the case—at Leavenworth. The English crowd, not expecting a fair shake, called another meeting.

This time the committee was presented with an intriguing suggestion from "Captain Jack" Goodman, a well-known local Civil War hero. Goodman suggested that the committee resign and turn the reins of leadership over to him. He would handle it his own way, and if it didn't work out, the committee wouldn't be responsible. Desperate times require desperate measures. Captain Jack was in charge.

Goodman organized a small army, consisting of about 100 two-horse wagons, 80 "cavalry," and 475 "infantry." Everyone met in English on Sunday, April 26, 1896, and Goodman drilled the horsemen until he was satisfied. About one o'clock in the morning, the long procession headed for Leavenworth.

Luther Turner, who was about twelve years old at the time, said many years later that he was watching as Goodman's army passed his home on South Main Street at the edge of town. He decided to go along and climbed aboard the last wagon. About two miles out of town, Captain Jack rode back on his horse to check on the wagons, saw young Luther, and asked him what he thought he was doing. "I'm going along to help out," Luther said. "Get off that wagon and get back to town!" said Goodman, in his best officer's voice. Luther said he still could remember that order and the long walk home.

Goodman's army completed the eighteen-mile trek and arrived in Leavenworth about seven o'clock that morning. The wagons circled the block in front of the courthouse and men were dispatched to bring the county officers from their homes to open the doors. Word of the raid had finally gotten out, but there was no time to organize any resistance to an armed force so large. The people of Leavenworth could only stand and watch as the wagons pulled up to the courthouse one at a time and loaded all the books, records, and even the furniture.

Everything was brought back to English—without incident—and stored in the brand-new stone building on the corner of Main and Fifth until the new courthouse was finished.

English was finally the county seat of Crawford County.

* * *

On Memorial Day, shortly before he died in 1916, Captain Jack Goodman recruited fifteen or twenty young boys, myself included, lined us up two abreast, gave us each an American flag, drilled us until he was satisfied, and marched us down Main Street as part of the festivities.

The Night Light

Volley Smith, who was born in 1886 and raised on a farm near Mifflin, told me that when he was about eighteen years old he heard of a bridge being built across the Ohio River at Louisville. They were paying three dollars a day, which was a lot of money for a kid who was used to working for twenty-five cents a day plus dinner.

Volley packed his things in his dad's old suitcase, walked to Taswell, and caught the train for Louisville. He arrived late in the afternoon and walked uptown. He said he had never seen such sights in all his life. He kept walking and gawking and staring at the tall buildings, the streetcars, the freight wagons, the fine horses and rubber-tired buggies, and the endless store windows with all kinds of fancy clothing and merchandise.

After eight or ten blocks of sightseeing, Volley realized that it was getting up into the shank of the evening and he had better start looking for a place to stay. Soon, he saw a sign that said ROOMS. He went in and discovered it was a saloon. The bartender was busy and told him to sit down and wait. There was a candy case nearby and Volley bought a nickel's worth in a small paper bag. (Back then, candy was always sold in bulk.)

Eventually, the bartender led Volley upstairs and down a long hallway. He opened a door, said, "This is your room," and left. The room was furnished with a bed, a dresser, and a couple of chairs. Hanging from the ceiling was a glowing electric bulb. Volley had heard about electric lights, of course, but this was the first one he had ever seen. This was every bit as impressive as the tall buildings and streetcars. Volley sat there in the room awhile, nibbled his candy, and thought about all the marvels he had seen that day.

Since he wanted to get up early the next morning to apply for the job on the bridge crew, Volley got ready for bed. He was tired from the long trip, but he couldn't seem to get to sleep.

The electric light was too bright.

Yes, there was probably a switch on the wall, and it was certainly connected to the light by a wire, and the bartender must have turned it on when he opened the door. But, having had no experience with things electrical, Volley was unaware of any of this. He lay there wide awake, staring at that devilish glowing bulb.

Finally, he got out of bed, stood on a chair, and looked the thing over. He blew on it several times, but the darn thing wouldn't go out. He went back to bed, but he still couldn't go to sleep. Something had to be done.

He happened to think of the candy sack. He emptied out the candy, got back up on the chair, and tied the sack over the light bulb. It worked. Volley finally got to sleep.

Well, fitfully, anyway. Every now and then he'd wake up and, sure enough, the light would still be there, glowing ominously under the candy sack.

When Volley got up the next morning, he was exhausted from rolling and tossing and lack of sleep. He decided right then and there that the big city was no place for a country boy. He packed his suitcase and headed back to Mifflin.

And left his candy sack on the electric light.

A Lesson Remembered

A boy who was raised near Fargo, about five miles north of English, and graduated from English High School in about 1908 told me this story.

When he was about twelve years old, he and his father walked to Marengo to attend the fair. He had worked all summer and had saved fifty cents. His father had two dollars—more than enough to pay for a full day of entertainment.

When they arrived at the fairgrounds, the first thing they saw was a man running a shell game. He had three shells and would place a pea under one of them, move them around, and then bet you couldn't guess which one the pea was under. It looked simple to the boy's dad, so he tried it and very quickly lost his two dollars.

But now he at least thought he had the game figured out. "Son, I know I can guess where the pea is. Give me your fifty cents."

Minutes later they were on their way home, broke. On the long trip back, his father told him, "Son, let that be a lesson to you. Never bet on the other man's game."

The boy was my second cousin, Monroe Melton. After high school, he graduated from the State Normal College at Terre Haute. He returned to English and was Superintendent of Schools for several years, then got advanced degrees from Indiana University and the University of Denver. When he retired in 1950, he was President of Illinois State Normal College.

He told me his trip to the Marengo fair with his father was expensive—a whole summer's wages—but he never forgot the lesson learned: *Never bet on the other man's game.*

Uncle Joe

My father and uncle were about twelve and thirteen years old when their mother died. Unable to work and raise two young boys, my grandfather left them with his wife's brother, Joe Lowe. Joe was well-known as a horse trader and often drank a little too much, but he was good to his young nephews and raised them as if they were his own.

Early one summer evening when I was about six or seven, a man stopped at our house leading Uncle Joe's horse with Uncle Joe just barely able to stay in the saddle. Usually when someone overindulged at the saloon it was only necessary to get him onto his horse and started toward home, knowing that the animal would find its way. But this method was only used on occasions when the rider seemed capable of not falling off somewhere in between. This was not one of those occasions. And, since Uncle Joe traded horses so often, you could never be sure exactly where he might end up. Better to deliver him directly to family.

We took him in, put him to bed, and Dad put his horse in the barn. A couple of days later I was playing in that bedroom and found a half pint of whiskey under the bed. Dad said he had heard Uncle Joe thrashing around that night and it must have been because he had lost his bottle and couldn't find it.

Roy Cummins, who was born in 1894, recently told me a story about Uncle Joe. Roy was about fourteen years old when it happened and said it was one of the biggest events in town during the horse and buggy days and was talked about for years afterwards.

No true horse trader ever trades for less than the most exceptional horse on the face of the entire planet, and on this day Joe was bragging that his new steed was the best step-climbing horse that he had ever seen. Boasts like this usually result in a wager, and soon Joe had covered bets from several of the boys who contended his horse couldn't climb the narrow hallway up to the lobby of the opera house.

No one said he had to ride the horse up the steps, so Joe went off to buy a box of feed, figuring to lead his horse up to victory. Word about events like this travels fast, and by the time Joe got back to the opera house, a crowd was gathering. Joe got in front of the horse and started coaxing him with the food. The first few steps weren't so bad, but as the crowd quickly grew and got more noisy, and as the stairwell got darker farther up, Joe's horse began to get skittish. About halfway up, Joe decided, bets or not, the horse was too spooked to continue. Since there wasn't room to turn around, Joe tried to get the horse to back down the steps. The poor creature seemed to like that idea even less. The only way down was up.

Maybe the horse was relieved at not having to go backward, and maybe it finally got into the spirit of the wager, but after only a little more coaxing and pulling, both Joe and the horse reached the lobby—and won the bet. The crowd cheered, Joe got his horse turned around, and . . .

Nothing. It was obvious the horse was not about to plunge into that dark, noisy downhill tunnel again. Ever. Joe pulled. Joe pushed. Joe coaxed, soothed, threatened, and even blindfolded the horse. Nothing.

Maybe Joe could have sold the horse right then and there on a sort of "as is" basis, but any deal he might have struck at that point would have been insulting to a horse trader like himself, so he decided to try the only option left: he called for help.

Joe sent for the veterinarian, who brought over a harness that was used to truss a horse up for castration. With help, they got the horse on its side, tied it up, and wrapped it in a blanket. Boards were laid on the steps and the horse was carefully slid down with ropes. Once on the street, it was unwrapped, untied, and resaddled, apparently none the worse for wear. By the time Joe paid for everything, he just about broke even.

Of course, he now owned a famous horse that he could sell for a nice profit—or trade for one that was even more exceptional.

1914

My family home still sits on Main Street, just north of the business district in English. I was born there on November 29, 1908, the fourth son of Alson and Anna Spears Roberts. My father owned a monument shop on Main Street for many years and I remember the business district well. Since much of what follows takes place on and around Main Street, it might be fun to take a walking tour of downtown English, Indiana as it used to be.

It's nine o'clock on a warm, sunny Saturday morning, July 18, 1914. We're standing at Main and Fifth in front of the Luckett Building. It's a big, two-story frame structure that was first built on Court Hill as a hotel, then bought by John Luckett and torn down and rebuilt here about a dozen years ago. The lower floor is the Turley Brothers' Hardware Store. Luckett's law office and some apartments are on the second floor.

The town is already busy and as we look down Main Street we can see several horse and mule teams tied to hitch racks. There's even a team of oxen. No automobiles are in sight, but there are five of them in town and we might see one before we finish our tour.

One thing we notice immediately is that Main Street isn't paved, it's dirt and gravel—muddy when it rains and dusty when it's dry. As a matter of fact, Thursday brought a welcome clod-soaking rain that put an end to the severe drought that had kept things dry—and dusty—for several weeks. The corn crop is saved and everyone is much relieved.

There's something unusual about the people on the street, and it's not just the old-fashioned look of the clothing styles from 1914. Women have those large, flowery hats, tiny corsetted waists, and long skirts that reach the ground. Because it's warm today, most men are in shirtsleeves and wear either a derby hat or a soft-looking felt fedora.

And that's what's so unusual. A quick glance around confirms it. *Everyone on the street is wearing a hat.* Everyone. Even some kids playing nearby are wearing straw hats that are almost identical except for the widths of the brims. Also, there are no bright colors in the clothing. Everything seems to be brown, black, or dark blue. Shirts are either blue or white. And, at least half or more of the men are wearing mustaches. The rest are clean-shaven. Beards only seem to be worn by the older men.

We could start walking south, crossing Fifth Street to the Crawford County State Bank, but it might be wise to wait just a moment. The old gentleman leaving the bank is D. W. Baggerly, a well-known retired farmer who has just recently built a new house in the west end. Whenever Dave sees strangers in town, he approaches them, introduces himself, and strikes up a conversation, always mentioning that he is a Democrat and a member of the Christian Church. Visitors in town always get noticed, but old Dave can be counted on to tell you their names, occupations, politics, church affiliations, and anything else of importance. Rather than try to explain who we are and how we got here, let's wait until he's across the street and headed for home.

The view east on Fifth shows a quiet, tree-lined street that is already a fast-growing residential area with some fine new homes. Like all the other streets off Main, it's dirt and gravel (mostly dirt) and in winter will be almost impassable after a hard freeze and thaw. A new, modern school building is also under construction up this way, right at the east edge of town. The contractor is confident that the work will be finished in time for the start of school in the fall (it won't). Weekly progress reports are printed in both of the town's newspapers. Speaking of progress, let's cross Fifth Street now.

The office of one of the newspapers, the *Crawford County Democrat,* is on the main floor in the back of the bank. On the upper floor are the Masonic Lodge and a dentist's office. This week's edition of *The English News,* the town's other paper, tells us that now is a good time to see the town at its best, since there has been "much work in the way of building concrete walls, painting residences, etc. More improvements have been made this summer than have been made in the past ten years altogether."

Beyond the bank is Boyd's Clothing Store and upstairs is the Modern Woodmen's Lodge. Next is Temple's Hardware, followed by the big platform where Ben Temple stores wire and fencing. Seated comfortably in a row of chairs in front of the hardware store are several of the town's retired citizens who congregate here to watch the goings-on. Most are veterans of the Civil War and receive monthly pensions.

They're looking forward to the annual Old Soldiers Reunion coming up in less than a month. Large crowds will gather at the Sloan property north of town for the event. Veterans of the War of the Rebellion always receive lots of recognition and never have to pay for anything.

This row of brick buildings behind them went through a disastrous fire just a few years ago, back in May, 1906. The fire was discovered about 12:30 A.M. in the rear of Boyd's Clothing Store. By the time the fire department arrived, the fire had gained such headway that it was uncontrollable. The bank, Boyd's store, and Temple's Hardware were completely gutted. Only an empty shell remained. The south wall of the hardware store was buckled and seemed about to collapse. After a few days, some carpenters went in, shored up the wall, and the buildings were rebuilt. The buckle caused by the fire is still there and is easy to see if we sight along the edge of the building. The deepest part of the sag is almost a foot.

Some of the horses tied nearby shift and snort nervously and we turn to see why. Here comes Charles "Paddy" Hughes, proudly putt-putting along in his grandfather's brand-new Reo motorcar. James Hughes bought the machine just last month and says it is "the best bargain that has been brought to English." (James's pride and joy—the Reo, not Paddy—will catch fire next week and be destroyed. He'll replace it with a Ford.) Most of the passersby stop to look at the shiny new car. Several kids run along behind.

Paddy is on his way to meet the morning trains, which will be arriving shortly. He picks up drummers (salesmen) and drives them to their appointments at country stores in Mifflin, Riddle, Temple, Grantsburg, Pumpkin Center, and Fargo. We get so interested watching Paddy and listening to his car that we almost miss another, even more important sound.

Clunk! Whack! We turn and get out of the way just in time. It's another well-known local merchant: "Blind" Connor. He's called "Blind" because he is, and instead of delicately tapping his way along with a cane, he clears his path by swinging a heavy six-foot walking stick. He's a big, husky fellow and it's obviously not a good idea to block his way.

Connor has been making his rounds, selling small, everyday

items like soap, spices, baking powder, and sewing kits door-to-door from the basket he carries. He goes all over town, stopping at each home, calling them by name and asking if they need anything. If someone gives him a bill and says it's a five or larger, he puts it in a pocket by itself and asks the next person he meets what it is.

Even the old boys in front of the hardware store abandon their chairs when they see Connor and his walking stick coming. They remember the day a farmer came to town, unloaded some logs, and carelessly left his empty wagon parked in such a way that Connor ran into it while making his rounds. Connor put down his basket and walking stick, turned the wagon on its side, and continued on.

Connor passes us and stops at the one-story frame building coming up on our left. The building has two business rooms, the first being the law office of S. A. Lambdin and the second being Connor's small grocery store. Cautiously, we walk past in the street as Connor unlocks the door. As soon as he is safely inside and we're out of his way, we step back up on the sidewalk.

Next is a two-story frame building with Brown's Barber Shop on the first floor. The sign in the window proudly advertises "A Clean Towel With Every Shave." Local businessmen also drop off their soiled stiff shirt collars here and "Hummer" Brown sends them to New Albany to be laundered and starched.

Up the wooden stairs, in the front room off the porch, is the Home Telephone Exchange, also owned by Brown. All local calls come through here. Long-distance calls have to be patched through the Southern Bell exchange over in the stone building. Quite a few people have telephones and pay the flat monthly rate of one dollar. English boasts 24-hour phone service, meaning the operator sleeps in the exchange, just in case.

As we pass Brown's Barber Shop, something new catches our attention: We can suddenly hear our footsteps. The concrete sidewalk has turned into a wooden boardwalk which leads onto the bridge crossing Camp Fork Creek. On our left, at the edge of the creek, is a one-story frame building occupied by *The English*

News and a business owned by a couple of entrepreneurs named Hankins and Stewart. James E. Hankins has a photography studio here, but he also sells jewelry and pianos. James Stewart is an attorney and sells Indian motorcycles. Together, they manage the opera house for its owner, Dr. Gobbel.

The bridge across the creek has wooden pedestrian walkways on each side. These are separate from the wagon bridge in the middle, which is about sixteen feet wide. We stop on the middle of the bridge and look upstream, realizing that the view is very different here in 1914. The creek bends sharply to our left, swinging over behind Brown's Barber Shop and *The News* office before curving back to flow under the bridge. In front of us is a big sawdust pile next to a mill where staves are sawed for whiskey barrels. The mill is powered by a steam engine and employs about fifteen men. The first building on the other side of the bridge is the brand-new Moore Building. Downstairs is a clothing store, a poultry house, and a saloon. Upstairs are living quarters.

I remember being with my uncle and following him into this saloon. Being a nosy little kid, I wandered into the wareroom in back while he stopped at the bar. There were some barrels standing on end and one empty barrel had the head knocked out and I stretched as far as I could to try to see inside it. My straw hat fell off and into the barrel. I wasn't big enough to reach in and get it, and I finally had to get my uncle to retrieve it for me.

Now we're at the railroad tracks and the Southern Depot. This is one of the busiest places in town. Six passenger trains run every day and people are always here to meet them. Some people just like to stop by and see who's getting on and off the trains. The busiest times are 9:30 A.M. and 6:00 P.M. This morning there are probably twenty people waiting for Trains #9 and #24. (Odd-numbered trains travel east and even-numbered trains travel west.) There are wagons unloading calves and cans of cream to be picked up by the eastbound train to Louisville. Someone from each of the two hotels is waiting to greet guests and carry their bags.

Many of the people are standing in the street, which at first seems odd and a little dangerous until we realize that not only is there almost no traffic, nothing on the street moves fast enough to surprise anybody anyway.

On the hill across the tracks south of the depot sits the home of Marshal Cummins. In April of 1907, the midnight train came through and the conductor told the marshal that some men had set fire to the railroad bridge at Temple. "Big Bill" went to investigate and found two men coming down the tracks. Shots were fired and Cummins was seriously wounded. He eventually recovered at a hospital in Louisville. The men who shot him are still at large.

As we cross Main Street, we notice the huge English Milling Company building just across the tracks. There's a small room under the south end of the adjacent warehouse where the town's fire-fighting equipment is stored. The total inventory consists of a pushcart with about 150 feet of fire hose. The fire department is whoever gets there first.

Farther south, at the corner of Main and Church, we can see what was one of my favorite hangouts—Landrus's Blacksmith Shop. Kids always seem to enjoy watching the smithy take the red-hot horseshoes out of the forge and shape them on his anvil to fit the horse's hoof. A good smithy can almost play a tune with his hammer and anvil.

Every summer, Dave Landrus would get a box of rings made out of horseshoe nails from a salesman and give them away to kids like me. They were always shiny at first, but they soon tarnished and left a dark circle around my finger.

The building back of the milling company is the light plant, which houses a D.C. generator powered by a big Fairbanks-Morris diesel engine. The generator is cranked up about dusk and shut down about eleven at night—or whenever the operator feels like leaving. This is okay since no one stays up past eleven anyway, and there are no electrical appliances of any kind. Customers pay a dollar per month—for each light bulb.

The street lights don't just blink off when the generator is shut down. They flicker and slowly dim, giving kids a few seconds to abruptly stop what they're doing and head for home. If I was playing near the tracks, the lights would be completely off before I could dash the length of Main Street. On a cloudy or moonless night, I would have to feel my way along the curb to get back.

We've crossed Main Street and are now in front of another saloon, this one owned by Joe Finch. Many of Joe's customers arrive and leave on horseback, and when these patrons have had a little too much to drink, Joe makes sure they get put on their horses and headed toward home. All they have to do is hang on and the horse will find the way. Next door to the saloon is Joe's home.

We cross the bridge on the other side and head back north. The first building across the creek is Lewis's Barber Shop. Jean Lewis gave my brother Clyde and me our first haircuts when we were about five and six years old. Clyde got so upset he jumped out of the chair and ran up the street with the barber's cape flapping around his neck.

The two empty lots now in front of us still show signs of the huge fire that consumed Alf Tillery's livery stable last year. Tillery's was a fine big frame building with stables and a hayloft. Also lost to the fire was the restaurant next door. It did a good business and was run by "Little Billy" Cummins, a distant relative of "Big Bill."

Next is a small frame dwelling that belongs to an old man named Mason who earns a good living making hickory canes which he sells for a quarter. His house sits at the edge of the sidewalk and Mr. Mason goes to bed when it gets dark. Some of the boys used to tease him by raking their pocket knives down the weatherboarding of his house and waking him up. They would laugh and run away when he came out to yell at them. One night the old man was waiting. He came out with a pistol and started shooting. The boys escaped down the street in a hail of bullets—and never teased the old man again.

The two-story building we're in front of now is especially memorable to me—my dad's monument shop. On display in the front room are several unlettered marble and granite monuments. In the back room is his workshop, where he hand-letters stones with a chisel and wooden mallet. Lettering one stone takes him the better part of a week. He also carves graceful vines, lambs, and doves for the more elaborate monuments.

Above Dad's shop are Chas. T. "Pekey" Brown's law office and the Odd Fellows Hall. The emblem of the Odd Fellows, three linked ovals with the letters F, L, T—Fellowship, Loyalty, and Truth—is displayed near the top of the storefront facade. It's painted gold and carefully carved out of wood (I think my father probably made it). The local kids say the letters stand for Fools, Liars, and Thieves.

We're back to Fifth Street now and on the corner is a one-story building with two business rooms. First is the butcher shop belonging to Rile Roberson. A local fellow named Cal Smith came into Rile's butcher shop one day with one of his mother's cured hams and sold it to Rile for drinking money. Shortly, Cal's mother came in and asked Rile if her son had sold him one of her hams. Rile admitted that he had. "Granny" Smith was furious and demanded that Rile return the ham, since he must have known why Cal wanted the money. Rile finally gave in and Granny wrapped the ham in her apron and went home. Some said that was the first time she had been downtown in twenty-five years.

The business on the corner is Patton & Hammond's Drugstore. Bill Patton is the proprietor of the drugstore and Felix Hammond, a dentist, is half owner. One Easter, after Sunday School, my dad and I stopped in here. I had a couple of colored Easter eggs. Dutch Benz said he would give me a nickel if I would crack one of the eggs on my dad's head. I looked up at Dad, who was sitting on a stool at the soda fountain. He smiled and pushed back his hat. I climbed up on the neighboring stool and cracked the egg on his forehead. Dutch laughed, gave me the nickel, and I bought an ice cream cone.

Let's turn left at the corner and walk west along Fifth Street. The first building after the drugstore is a one-story frame building with two business rooms. First is a grocery and meat market run by Charley Rosenbarger. When I was about eight years old, Guido Patton and I came down the alley back of Rosenbarger's and saw a fellow named Levi Brown rendering lard in a big iron kettle. We decided to hang around until Levi used the lard press, so we could get some cracklins. Levi must have been drinking, because he staggered and fell into an empty kettle that was turned on its side. When he tried to get out, the kettle rolled and he kept falling back. He asked us to help him, but we were afraid and ran. I never did find out how Levi got out of that kettle.

Next is a shoe repair shop run by a little hunchback fellow named Fred Weil. Beyond that is a restaurant owned by George Dooley. Dooley sold watermelons for ten cents, and my friend Henry Smith and I used to chip in a nickel each, take our melon down to the creek on a hot summer day, and eat it in the shade with our feet dangling in the cool water.

In the alley next to Dooley's restaurant, we notice several kids playing a favorite game, ring marbles. They've taken a stick and drawn a circle on the ground about five feet across, with a small, six-inch ring in the middle. Each kid has put three or four small marbles—called peadads—in the center ring. The object is to "knuckle down" at the edge of the big circle and shoot at the peadads with a bigger marble called a taw. Peadads knocked out of the big circle are kept by the shooter. This is known as "playing for keeps."

The kid about to take his turn as shooter is Billy Moore. He's one of the best shots around and uses a special taw called an agate. It's a brownish, cloudy color and if we could hold it up to the light we'd see half moons in it. Billy is very particular with his agate and won't let anyone else shoot with it. Just as he knuckles down, one of the other boys accuses him of "fudging," meaning some part of his hand was over the line. He denies it, and an argument starts. We continue on, knowing that the worst that will happen is some loud cussing—no one ever fights over something like that.

Beyond the alley is a three-story brick hotel built in 1902 by a man named Lee Cotner. A few years ago he sold it to A. F. "Dad" Colebaugh, who is now the proprietor.

The offices of the Hammond Brothers, Felix and Guido, are next. Felix is the dentist who co-owns the drugstore and Guido is a doctor. They were the first in town to own an automobile—a brand new Ford Model T—and Felix takes it out for a spin most every evening after work. I got my first automobile ride one evening in that Model T.

Now we're in front of the post office. This very spot was the scene of a recent incident which has caused great consternation locally. Two young ladies on their way home were pelted with eggs by unknown assailants. This kind of behavior is not taken lightly and the *Democrat,* in a front-page article entitled "This is the Limit!," called upon the parents of the perpetrators to "administer the good old-fashioned home treatment"—a good, hard strapping in the woodshed.

Across Water Street is the barber shop of Henry Perkins, who is also a well-known horse trader. As we turn north, "Perk," who probably weighs in at around three hundred pounds, leaves his shop talking with a potential customer, headed for his nearby barn. We overhear something about "best horse in the county" as they walk away, leaving a half-shaved customer in the barber chair.

Across Fifth on the corner is Harve Heishman's ten-cent store. Harve lives upstairs and handles just about anything you could want. My favorite was the foot-long piece of licorice candy he sold for a penny. Heishman's sells a dozen peadads for a nickel, but you can usually buy three dozen from Billy Moore for the same price.

Next as we go north on Water Street is a one-story frame building with two business rooms. The first room is a millinery shop run by Della Byrd. The window is full of the kinds of hats we saw uptown, with wide brims and lots of flowers. The grocery store next door belongs to a one-legged man named Iny Dooley. Iny was our neighbor when I was a kid, and he would lay down his crutches and challenge my brother and me to stand on one leg longer than he could. We never won. One time Iny asked us if we had ever been to Brownstown, about four miles north. We hadn't, so he proceeded to tell us about the streetcars that ran there and the orange trees that grew in the streets. I went to my dad, anxious to go to this wonderful place. Dad just smiled and said not to believe everything Iny said.

The house beyond Iny's store belongs to State Senator Sam Benz, who also owns the clothing store next door. His store was built in 1896 and was the first brick building in English. I came here with my mother one time and she left me to play in front of the store. Charley Benz and Major Conn were sitting outside and pointed across the street to a big white rooster and a couple of hens. Charley said he would give me a nickel if I would catch that rooster. When I went after him, he jumped on me, knocked me down, and was giving me a pretty good thumping until Charley and Major came to my rescue. I didn't catch the rooster and never got the nickel.

Across Fourth Street and on the corner is the Commercial Hotel, a big two-story frame building. The owner is W. C. Walker. I became pretty good buddies with Walker's grandson, Wayne, who lived about thirty miles away and always visited for a month or two during the summer. When we were about fifteen, Wayne snitched a couple of cigars from the hotel office and we hid in the coal house out back and smoked them. We were enjoying our cigars when his grandmother opened the coal house door and caught us. I jumped out the window and ran up the alley. A couple of days later, my brother Clyde, who was eighteen months older but about my size, was passing the hotel. The grandmother, who was sitting on the porch, grabbed him. "I'll teach you to get my Wayne to steal cigars!" And Clyde got a good thrashing that was meant for me. I was probably lucky he didn't pass it along.

Across Water Street is the small frame building where my dad started his monument business in 1898. He moved up on Main Street in about 1908.

As we head back south, we notice a fine-looking horse and

rubber-tired buggy stopped at the watering trough on the corner. It's driven by William E. Moore (no relation to Billy), another Civil War veteran who is a lifelong resident of English. It would be fun to stop and talk to him because when he moved here the town was just a few log cabins and many of the early settlers—like James Sloan—were still alive.

During the week, Bill can usually be found sitting on one of the benches along Main Street. He likes to tell about how he tried to enlist in the Union Army when he was only fifteen. The recruiter told him he was too young for a soldier, but signed him up as a drummer boy. After a couple of battles, he threw away his drum, picked up a rifle from a fallen soldier and fought until he was hit by a minnie ball that tore away part of his left arm and ended his army career. If you ask, he'll be glad to give you all the details and even show you his scar.

The two-and-a-half-story home with the big yard across from Benz's store belongs to Dr. Fred R. Gobbel, who moved here from Grantsburg a few years ago. Behind Dr. Gobbel's house is the barn where he keeps his horses and buggy to make house calls. In the barn is a locked room that you can get into by climbing up through the hayloft. Inside the room are saddles, harness, tools, and a wooden box about six feet long with a hinged lid. Inside the box is a skeleton.

Most of the boys around enjoy taking other kids to see the skeleton, known as "Old Joe." No one knows for sure where Joe came from, but there are several big tales told about his origin. My favorite is that he was a wino found dead by the tracks. Dr. Gobbel supposedly hired another couple of winos to take the body out into the woods and boil the meat off the bones. It took them three days to do it and the smell was terrible.

Now we're back to Fifth Street and we turn east, toward Main. Across the alley is a two-story brick building also owned by Dr. Gobbel. The first of the three business rooms is his office and the second is a drugstore run by his son, Nova. The third space is where Steve Patton has his general store.

The narrow stairwell beyond Patton's leads up to the opera

house. (This is where Uncle Joe Lowe and his step-climbing horse became famous.) Stage shows, revivals, graduations, and the like are held here. Movies are shown twice a week. The screen is a white sheet hung on the wall and the projector is cranked by hand. At the end of each reel—about every ten minutes—they turn on the house lights and rethread the projector while people sit and talk.

There's a stairwell at the back of the opera house that's used as a fire escape. If you lay a board between the stairs and the roof of Dr. Gobbel's office—which is only one story—you can sneak across and watch the shows through the opera house windows for free.

We hear some commotion from across the street and see that Nova Gobbel has joined the boys playing marbles. He doesn't play himself, but just bets on the shooters and gives odds. He knows the skills of the players pretty well and usually leaves with more marbles than he came with.

Now we're back to Main Street and the two-story stone building built by Dr. C. D. Luckett in 1896. Dr. Luckett is the brother of John, who built the Luckett Building across the street. The Condra Brothers took the contract to lay the sandstone blocks for $1000. Before the job was finished, they went broke and Dr. Luckett had to hire someone else to complete the job. The building was first used to store the county records and hold court while the courthouse was under construction. Dr. Luckett's office and the Southern Bell telephone exchange are upstairs. On the first floor is Charley Crews's General Store. Charley handles a complete line of yard goods, shoes, and groceries and also buys poultry and eggs. In the fall he specializes in sorghum and sorghum barrels. He'll sell you a new suit for $3.50, but his best all-wool suits go for $10 and $15.

We hear the whistle of an approaching train in the distance. Several people leave the drugstore and other businesses and hurry toward the depot. Only the Civil War vets in front of the hardware store don't seem interested.

It's been a long, hot walk, so we take a welcome drink from the continuously-flowing sulfur well on the east side of the stone building, right at the edge of the street.

Refreshed, we cross Main Street again and notice that the Luckett Building, where we began our tour, has been replaced by a parking lot for a new post office. Behind us, a truck rumbles past. We turn, and realize that the dusty streets, hitching posts, teams of horses, and all but a few landmarks are once again far behind us.

Schools and the Superintendent

In 1914, a fine, new, modern brick school was built at the east edge of town. It had four rooms down, four rooms up, and a full basement. Construction problems delayed the opening for almost a month, but when the new building was finally ready on October 12, I was there to start my schooling. I was not quite six years old.

Dad took my brother Clyde and me that first day and we had to wait in front until the doors opened at eight o'clock. The building seemed really big and I was scared. Leo Land was a junior in high school and suddenly announced that he was tired of waiting for school to open and that he was going to break down the doors. He stepped back, took off his hat, and rushed toward the double doors like a charging football player, stopping only at the last second. I thought he meant it, and I was *really* scared.

My great-uncle, Jesse Melton, taught the first and second grades, so that helped some. At noon, Dad came back, got Clyde

> It will not be long until the schools of our county will open up, and many a child will be hustled off, even before it is old enough, just to get rid of it. If the teachers will do their duty all such will be kindly sent home to their parents.

Crawford County Democrat, September 3, 1914

and me together, and brought our lunch in a Blue Granite bucket. After a few days of that, I took my own dinner bucket (we didn't call them lunch pails). Before long, I was looking forward to school every day.

* * *

I made straight A's in the first and second grades, but before I started the third grade one of the older kids told me how tough the teacher, Miss Marie Goodwin, was. I decided to be just as tough as she was, and as a result, we didn't hit it off too well.

We had double seats and Herb Walls was my seat partner. We found some boxes that had been used for bolts and nuts and decided they would make good pencil boxes. Since our desk wasn't big enough for both books and boxes, we stacked our books on the floor so we could put our fancy pencil boxes in our desk. Of course, Miss Marie told us we couldn't do that and to get rid of the boxes.

I smarted off about getting a burlap bag for our books and she gave me a whack on the jaw. Our relationship went downhill from there. It wasn't long before Herb and I were taking turns getting whipped with Miss Marie's leather strap and competing to see who could get the worst grades.

Marie was young and high-tempered—something we had in common—and I believe if she had just sat me down and talked things over she might have gained my confidence and we could

—PHOTO BY ARMSTRONG

NEW JOINT HIGH SCHOOL BUILDING FOR ENGLISH AND STERLING TOWNSHIP.

The new school building, recently completed and now in use, is 49 feet, 3 inches wide; 7[illegible] feet, 8 inches long, and 43 feet in height. Total cost $12,350, not including furniture.

Crawford County Democrat, October 29, 1914

have gotten along. As it was, I didn't start making the kinds of grades I was capable of making until sixth grade.

(Miss Marie spent her entire career at English. When my son, Nick, started second grade in 1950, Miss Marie was still there. They, however, hit it off from the very beginning, and she was one of his favorite teachers.)

* * *

One of my classmates and a good friend in the eighth grade was Seth Denbo. Regardless of what he did, Seth always worked hard to be a winner. That included not wasting time. As soon as the noon hour began, Seth would eat his lunch as fast as he could—usually a couple of sandwiches in a paper bag—and rush to the playground for his favorite pastime, baseball.

One fall day was particularly hot and sticky. When books took up at the end of the noon hour, Seth came running in at the last minute, soaking wet. I was sitting in the same row as Seth, in the last seat. Bill Reasor was in front of me, then Seth, then Lee Strothers. Leonard Cummins was our teacher and he had just started class when I heard a short, deep, gurgle from in front of me. I looked up just in time to see Seth struggling to get his red bandana out of his pocket. Before he could cover his mouth, he threw up all over Lee—down his back and in his hair. We were all so shocked we just stared in silence as Lee slowly stood up with his arms spread out, covered with the remains of Seth's lunch. Bill turned to me.

"Looks like Seth had cheese for lunch."

"And he didn't chew it very well, either."

Mr. Cummins led Seth and Lee out of the room and downstairs to the rest room, leaving a trail behind them. They both took the rest of the day off.

(Seth didn't lose his fighting spirit. He built a successful hatchery and feed business and was elected Republican Chairman of the Eighth District in 1962, a position he held until his death in 1985.)

* * *

The superintendent of schools at this time—and the one I remember most—was S. A. Beals. Beals set the rules and expected everyone to obey them. He told us he was in charge from the time we left home in the morning until we got back home in the afternoon.

Two of his rules were: *No smoking on school property or on the way to and from school.* And, *Stay on the sidewalks and don't run through people's yards.* One morning a friend of mine, Kenneth Luckett, was about five minutes late and at the end of Fifth Street he cut across a yard to save time. When he walked in the front door of the school, Superintendent Beals was there to meet him.

"Kenneth, I saw you run through Mrs. Brown's yard. Go back there and apologize right now." Kenneth went back down to Mrs. Brown's, told her what he'd done, said he was very sorry and that he would never do it again.

And he didn't.

One of the high school boys, Russell Megenity, came to town one night in the middle of the week and happened to meet Mr. Beals on the street.

"Russell, you know your grades aren't too good. You should be home studying." Russell immediately headed for home and from then on only came into town on weekends.

In about 1927–28, English had a pretty good basketball team. Somewhere on the way to a game at Bedford, the boys picked up some moonshine whiskey, and by game time they were feeling pretty good. It must have helped; they won the game. One of the boys who ran up a pretty good score said it was hard to miss when he could see three baskets to shoot at. In spite of the victory, when word of the drinking incident reached Superintendent Beals, he immediately canceled the rest of the year's basketball schedule.

I was known as the school artist, and after the schedule was canceled, I drew a cartoon of a little fellow with a big head that looked like a basketball with big eyes and ears. He was wearing an EHS basketball jersey and straddling Lawrence County, with Bedford, the county seat, under his feet. He was waving a bottle with XXX on it. The caption was: "The Winner!" I gave the drawing to Mr. Beals's son, Orman, who was also a student. The next day at school I met Mr. Beals in the hall and he pulled the drawing out of his coat pocket. I thought I was about to get chewed out. He looked at the cartoon and started laughing. And laughing. And laughing. He actually laughed till he cried, then finally complimented me on the drawing. I felt a lot better.

A friend of mine named Wathan Leasor was caught smoking by a teacher and was marched to Mr. Beals's office, where he was expelled. When he went home and told his mother what had happened, she decided to take matters into her own hands. She was related to Guido Hammond, who was on the school board, so she went to him and complained that Superintendent Beals had expelled her son. Guido said, "We hired Beals to run that school and if it gets to where he can't run it, we'll get someone else." And with that, he turned and walked away.

S. A. Beals became superintendent when I was in about the fifth grade and was still there when I finished my schooling.

(Beals had come to English after being an attorney and the *County* Superintendent of Schools at a time when many rural parents were illiterate and did not appreciate the value of an education. He worked tirelessly to promote reading skills and encourage teachers in the most remote one-room schools. He was the youngest ever to hold that office.)

Grandfather Spears

In the summer of 1914, my dad hired a team and surrey from Hughes Livery Stable for a trip to see my grandfather, Nathan Spears. He lived in a log house near Fargo, about seven miles from English. In those days, travelers followed the creek beds through the bottoms, and dirt roads on higher ground. Traveling was either bumpy, dusty, and miserable or, when it rained, wet, muddy, and miserable.

A trip like that was pretty much an all-day affair, with just the round trip taking about four hours. When we arrived at Grandfather's house, he and the family came out to greet us. I remember that he opened the barnlot gate for us and helped Dad unhook the team. I still remember the old log house. The downstairs consisted of a living room with a big fireplace, and a couple of smaller rooms. A steep, narrow stairway led to a couple of bedrooms upstairs. There was a big back porch.

The next morning, Clyde and I went with Uncle Willis to water the horses. There was a lane from the barn to a spring down the hill. The water flowed into a basin hewed out of sandstone where it was dipped out for household use. The overflow went to a horse trough made from a hollow log. It was always fun going to Grandpa's and playing in the old log barn or exploring in the woods. We could always find something to do.

On the trip back, we hadn't gone very far when it started pouring rain. After a couple of miles we were in the bottoms following the creek, and the water kept getting higher, at times coming up in the surrey bed. Then we got out onto higher ground for a couple of miles until the road forded the creek. The water was swift and it was getting dark. Dad said that if we could get across, we would be out of the water the rest of the way home.

We sat there for some time, but the water kept rising. Dad finally decided we should try to find a place to stay the night, so we turned around and took another road up the hill for about a half mile and stopped at a farm. Dad asked the farmer if he could put us up for the night. He said he didn't have enough room, but Jerry Carter, who lived at the top of the hill, had a big house and would take us in.

It was dark by the time we got to the Carter farm and they were in bed. Dad got them up and Carter said he would be glad to keep us. He took care of our team and we all went in. Carter's wife and granddaughters got out of bed and fixed us supper, then showed us where to sleep. Next morning, we had breakfast, hooked up the team, thanked them, and headed for home.

(One of Carter's granddaughters was Irene Conn. A few years ago when she was about seventy-five, I mentioned the incident to her and she said she remembered getting out of bed that night and coming downstairs to help fix our supper. She was about sixteen.)

About a year later Grandfather Spears was bad sick. My uncle, Adison Spears, came in on the train from his home in Provo, Utah. My dad hired a horse and buggy to take him to see Grandpa and I went along.

I remember Grandpa in bed by the fireplace, in a lot of pain. When Dad and I got ready to leave, Grandpa told my step-grandmother to "get Everett some of those hickory nuts." I guess he wanted to give me something and that was all he could think of. Grandma brought me a small sack of nuts and I took them home. My mother told me I should put some of them away and keep them. She probably knew he wouldn't be here long.

About three days later one of Grandpa's neighbors arrived on horseback about daybreak with the bad news: Grandpa Spears had passed away. That was June 15, 1916. Just five days after his seventy-fourth birthday.

Reunions

The first English Reunion was in 1887. It was called the Old Soldiers Reunion and for several years was held on the farm of George W. "Dutch" Sloan, James Sloan's son and a local veteran of the Civil War.

The early Reunions were daytime affairs, since most people had to get home by dark to do chores. Even the local people left before dark. About all that went on at night was a square dance, attended mostly by the rough element.

The Reunion lasted all week and people came for miles to attend. They came in wagons, in buggies, on horseback, by foot, and on the train. The old Civil War veterans were guests of honor and they would camp out on the grounds for the first three days. There was a tent with bunks and tables and they cooked meat, beans, and potatoes outside in big kettles.

The big day was Thursday and the town would be full of people. The livery stable operated a hack, driven by Jim Hughes, which was a wagon with a canopy top. It had steps at the rear and benches along the sides. It was pulled by a big team with bells on the harness. There would usually be a line of people waiting at the depot when Jim would stop and yell, "Hack for the ground!" The fare was five cents one way.

The Civil War veterans borrowed an old brass cannon from a veterans organization in Tell City. It was shipped in on a railroad car and pulled by a team of horses to a location on the hill above the Reunion grounds. Early every morning, the veterans would load and fire the cannon.

John Bay Smith, who moved to English from Valeen in about 1850, told me about a couple of fellows who had had a few drinks and were on their way to the Reunion ground. As they passed by the cannon they noticed that the powder, wadding, and ramrod were nearby, so they decided to load and fire it themselves. They poured in the powder, tamped it good with wadding, and fired the cannon. Only then did they realize that they had forgotten to remove the ramrod and it was now somewhere out in the valley. John Bay Smith was the one who found it sticking out of the ground in the middle of his cornfield that fall.

* * *

I remember the Reunion of 1916. My dad had a new Overland Touring Car, and at that time there were only seven or eight automobiles in town. It had rained on and off all week, and on Thursday afternoon it came a downpour. Dad decided to run a taxi service from the grounds. I went with him, and when we arrived, there were several young women standing under a big beech tree, soaking wet. Several of them made a dash for our car. I remember them trying to keep their long skirts out of the mud and how their big flowery hats drooped down to their shoulders from the weight of the water. We took them into town and made several more trips. I think Dad charged a dime.

The "Baby Rack" or "Doll Rack" always had a big crowd of onlookers. The object was to win a kewpie doll by knocking stuffed cats with weighted bottoms off a shelf at the back of the booth with the three balls you got for a dime. You could win a small kewpie doll if you knocked off two cats and a larger, much nicer doll if you knocked off three. All the young fellows with girlfriends always tried hard to win one of the nicer dolls. It seemed to help business when the game was run by a good-looking girl.

I had my fortune told by the gypsy fortune-teller, but she talked so much and so fast that I never really understood anything she was saying. I haven't been to one since.

As Curtis "Buggy" Lone was leaving the fortune-teller's tent, he saw two women who, like himself, were also from the Grantsburg area. He knew they didn't believe in fortune-tellers, so he pointed them out to the gypsy and told her all about them. He then told the ladies that he had been to the fortune-teller and was

BIG EVENT

Of Year In English Is In Full Blast.

The big event of the year in English, the one looked forward to from one year to another, has again rolled around and this week the twenty-seventh annual Soldiers Reunion is in full blast. This year the reunion is also home coming week for former citizens and many of these, who have taken up their abode in other parts of the country have arrived in English during the past few days. At the reunion each year old acquaintances are renewed and friends, who have not met for years, are reunited.

It was thought the rain first of the week would dampen the enthusiasm of the crowd somewhat but all are seemingly well entertained On the grounds, north of town, there is a great crowd of merry-makers each day. The steam swing, fish fry, "baby rack," fortune teller, with lemonade, ice cream and cracker jack, are receiving their undivided attention. Veterans of the Civil War are meeting, old comrades are again clasping hands but their ranks are thinner each year.

The English News, August 4, 1916

amazed at what she had known about him. They didn't agree to go until Buggy promised to refund their money himself if they weren't as amazed as he had been. And, of course, they were. It was the highlight of the week for them and they talked about it long after the Reunion was over. Buggy told me that he never did tell them how she had done it.

* * *

The last Reunion at the Sloan farm was in 1917. One of the shows that fascinated me that year was the Spider Girl. The picture on the tent showed a girl's head with a spider's body, and there was also a barker out front describing her and trying to convince passersby that one dime was a small price to pay to see such a marvel.

My dad usually gave me a quarter for the day and I tried to make it go as far as possible. Ten cents out of my quarter seemed like a lot, but I had to find out if this was possible. Sure enough, inside was a huge spider with a real girl's head on it. She would even laugh and talk to you while you watched. As we used to say then, it was the beatin'est thing I had ever seen. I stayed a long time and got my dime's worth.

Another memorable attraction on the grounds that year was a hootchie-cootchie show. There was a scantily-clad girl out front walking back and forth on a platform, and above that was a viewing area about eight feet square with a railing around it. For a quarter (!) you could stand at the railing, look down into the tent, and watch the girl dance—on a mirror (!!). No kids were allowed into this show, but it didn't make any difference since I only had fifteen cents left after the Spider Girl anyway.

A lot of young fellows were crowded around the railing to see the first show. Among them was the county sheriff, Dale Hammond, in civilian clothes. As soon as it was over, Hammond walked over to the barker, showed his badge, and closed down the show. I remember the barker arguing with the sheriff, but it didn't do any good. That was the Reunion's first and last hootchie-cootchie show.

The next day, the show reopened. Instead of a dancing girl in the pit, there was now a live alligator. A fellow would hit the alligator on the nose with a stick and it would bite the stick in two. That, I went to see. It only cost a nickel.

The only ride at the Reunion in those early years was the Steam Swing. It was a merry-go-round with steel wheels that ran on a flat track and was pulled by a big cable attached to a steam engine that sat next to it. It played music and each ride was a nickel.

There was a boy named Gregory who somehow always managed to get the job of carrying water from the nearby spring for the steam engine. All of the other boys envied him because he got to ride for free. He would wait until the swing was going full speed and then hop on. The steam engine only used one bucket of water about every hour. Not a bad job.

(The Steam Swing was always located in the same place on the hill at the Sloan farm and the ashes from the steam engine accumulated over all the years the Reunion was held there. The remnants of the ash pile remained until Highway 64 came through in the early sixties.)

* * *

In 1900, the son of William H. English gave the town a statue of his father. It was set up on land that was donated to the town for a park, but for years the land was never cleaned or developed. When I first remember the park, a farmer had corn growing there. When the corn was full-grown, it just covered the base of the statue and left Mr. English standing all alone on top of a green and gold carpet.

In the main part of the park were several big virgin beech trees. The sulfur well made a swamp full of cattails that we used to wade in. The water was six to eight inches deep and was always cold, even in July.

When William Rice brought the basket factory to English in 1921, he got the Town Board interested in the park. As a result, the board appointed a park committee, and with donations of labor and money, the "grove west of town" was cleaned up.

Benches were set up around several of the big trees. Rope swings were put up for the kids and glider swings were provided for the older people. The sulfur well was cleaned out and cased with new pipe that extended about three feet above the ground. Four half-inch pipes ran refreshing streams of water.

There was no Reunion in 1918 because of the World War. In 1919, the Reunion was moved to the William Gilliland farm and was held there for two years. In 1921, the Reunion was moved to the new park and has been held there ever since. As fewer and fewer old soldiers returned each year—the Spanish-American and World War veterans were still young—the "Old Soldiers Reunion" slowly became known as just the "English Reunion."

The Fly Drive

Flies were always a problem in the summer, but especially on the farms. Having a barn, a hog pen, a chicken house, and a manure pile nearby meant a concentration of the pests available to infest the kitchen. The only barrier between inside and outside was a screen door, which was open most of the time anyway as the kids ran back and forth. When there was company and a big meal was prepared, it could seem like there were more flies indoors than out.

It was time for the fly drive.

Two or three women would get towels or diapers and start fanning and shooing the flies from the opposite end of the room. Someone would be stationed to open the door as they approached and let the flies out. Two or three passes like this usually got rid of most of the intruders. What few were left could be fanned off the food during the meal.

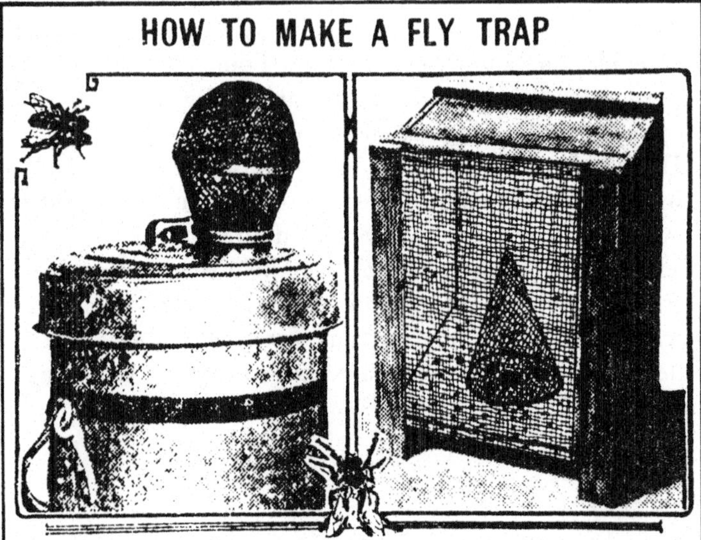

HOW TO MAKE A FLY TRAP

Get a soap box of large size. Substitute wire netting for the top and two sides. Cut a round hole in the bottom and insert in it a wire netting cone with a one-eighth-inch opening at the bottom and a half-inch opening at the top. Place a fish head or piece of food inside for bait. Elevate the trap a few inches from the ground so the flies may enter. When the trap is crowded, kill the flies with boiling water

The English News, April 28, 1916

Dad had a trap almost exactly like the one on the right. He used molasses for bait but I don't think he did anything to kill the flies—they just died of old age. And yes, the trap worked pretty well.

Threshing Time

Before tractors, most farmers worked their crops with about two horsepower. Twenty-five to thirty acres of corn was a typical yield. Since corn was only "knee high by the Fourth of July," some farmers also planted eight or ten acres of wheat, which could be harvested sooner. July was wheat threshing time and when the threshing crew came to set up, several of us kids were always there to watch.

A man named Bill Brubeck did most of the threshing in the area. He had a big self-propelled Case steam engine that he and his crew drove from farm to farm. It chugged along at about two miles an hour—which made it easy for us kids to follow—and pulled the actual thresher or separator behind it.

The steam engine was huge and heavy, and when it had to cross over a bridge or a culvert the crew would check to see if it was safe. One of the most exciting things about following them was waiting to see if the steam engine would break through. (A different steam engine actually did break through the Dog Creek bridge once—and we missed it. I remember seeing it on its side in the creek. Fortunately, no one got hurt.)

Brubeck always set up his steam engine near the barn and it had to be level so the big belt that ran from it to the thresher would stay on. The engine used a lot of water, and a horse-drawn water wagon was a necessary piece of additional equipment.

The water wagon was a wooden boxlike tank on wheels and had a two-cylinder pump on top. The pump had a handle about three feet long that had to be pulled back and forth. The driver would stop in the creek, drop a suction line into the water, and fill up. The tank probably held three or four hundred gallons and it took about fifteen minutes to fill.

Usually, we either volunteered or got recruited to do the pumping, and I remember pulling and pushing with another kid while the driver sat back and bragged on how fast we could fill the tank.

Workers in the field followed a horse-drawn binder, which cut the wheat, tied it, and left it on the ground in bundles. They stacked the bundles in piles of about a dozen each, which were hauled to the thresher on a wagon.

The binder was a relatively new invention, replacing a back-breaking and exhausting job called cradling, where a worker with a scythe cut a swath of wheat, scooped it up into the crook of one arm, and used several of the wheat straws to tie it into a bundle. I knew an old-timer named "Bill-Dad" Brown who told me his claim to fame as a young man was that he could cradle more wheat in a day than anyone else. "They always tried to keep up with me," he said proudly, "but they never could."

Back at the thresher, two of the crew were kept busy cutting open the bundles of wheat and spreading them out so they fed smoothly into the mouth of the thresher. A fireman kept the boiler hot and the water wagon was always making trips back and forth to the creek. A mechanic was there to keep everything running smoothly. Another man bagged the grain after it was separated from the straw.

The straw blew out of a tall L-shaped pipe and made a pile nearby. After a hard day of following the steam engine, pumping water, and watching the crew set up, it was fun to unwind by playing in the straw pile as soon as it was big enough.

Bill Brubeck paid his men seventy-five cents a day, which included a free meal—usually a sumptuous feast—prepared by the owner of the farm. Bill never had a problem finding workers.

Horseless

The first automobile came to English in 1912. It was owned by a relative of Charley Rosenbarger's, who drove in to visit. Everyone in town wanted to ride in it, so Rosenbarger advertised that he would be out at the Jim Tucker farm near the grove west of town on the following Sunday and would take passengers for twenty-five cents each.

A track was laid out in one of Tucker's fields, and when Sunday arrived, so did about three hundred people, all eager to pay their quarter and have a new experience. This was one of those times when it was wise to be first in line. After about two laps, the car broke down and that—since no one had the slightest idea how to fix it—was that. Everyone went home using the same reliable four-legged transportation they were familiar with.

Despite all the interest, it was two years before someone in English bought an automobile. The Hammond brothers purchased a brand-new Ford Model T in 1914. They kept it in a barn near our home and every evening after Dr. Felix Hammond closed his dental office he would take it out for a spin. There were always five or six of us kids who were ready and eager to go along. That was how I got my first automobile ride.

Most people spoke of these early automobiles as "machines" and very few people knew anything about what made them go. My dad bought a new Overland in 1916, and I remember once when he had trouble with it, he called Jenner's garage at Marengo. They sent a mechanic by the name of Burtie Burton on the morning train. He spent about ten minutes adjusting the carburetor, then charged Dad five dollars. This left Burtie plenty of time to visit relatives before leaving town on the evening train.

Most all early automobile owners had their own fifty-gallon storage tanks for gasoline. About once a month a Standard Oil tank wagon—pulled by a team of horses—would come by to fill them.

Back then people weren't concerned with mileage, they thought more about power and would brag on their car's ability to pull hills. On the Model T the carburetor was gravity-fed, meaning the gas tank was higher than the carburetor so the gas would flow down to it. If a hill was too steep, the car would quit. The solution was to turn around and back up the hill.

* * *

Model T's were not designed for the impatient, and I'm not just talking about their top speed. Here's how you start one and drive it away: There's a hand crank in front. If the coils and spark plugs are in good shape, the car will generally start on a quarter-turn. This is also something to brag about. If not—as is usually the case—it takes a lot of cranking and a little cussing to get it going.

If the spark control is set too high—that's the lever on the left side of the steering column—the crank can snap back and break your arm. This is known as a "Ford fracture" and results in even more cussing.

The gas lever—on the right side of the steering column—should be set just high enough to make the car start properly (something learned from experience).

Assuming that you set the spark and the gas properly, and that the car starts with a few choice words and no injuries, you can get behind the wheel—from the passenger side, since there is no door on the driver's side—and immediately increase the spark so the engine won't die. (Some drivers prefer to jump over the fake door to reach the spark more quickly.) By the way, the reason there's no door on the driver's side is because the emergency brake is in the way.

You set the emergency brake prior to cranking so the car wouldn't run over you when you started it (didn't you?), so now you step on the clutch, which is the foot pedal on the left—there are *three*—and at the same time grip the emergency brake and release it by squeezing the handle.

Pushing the clutch in doesn't take the transmission out of gear, it puts it into low, the slower of the two forward speeds. Releasing the emergency brake engages the transmission and starts the car forward. Give it a little more gas, get some speed, and let the clutch out. Now you're in high gear and on your way. The gas lever controls your speed.

The foot pedal on the right is the brake. Be sure to push in the clutch if you slow down and pull on the hand brake if you have to stop. By the way, if you want to back up, press the reverse pedal (the one in the middle) and let off on the hand brake.

A whole new dimension is added to the above when it's cold, dark, or raining. When it gets dark, there are electric lights, but, since they run off the car's magneto, they get very dim when the car slows down. The windows have snap-on isinglass curtains that roll up and fit under the seat, but they always crack and at least two or more of the snaps on each curtain never work.

I learned all these driving techniques—sort of—by watching. When I was about sixteen, Zenor Brown told me he had to take a team of horses back to his dad's farm north of town and asked me if I would drive his Model T so he could have a ride back. This was my first opportunity to drive—Dad wouldn't let me—so of course I said yes.

Everything went smoothly until the Model T started moving. It would speed up for a few yards and then drag down when I let out the clutch. I'd push it back in, get some speed, and as soon as I tried for high gear, CHUGA-CHUGA-CH-CH-CHUG . . .

It was about two miles to the farm and I drove the whole way in ten-yard spurts. I told Zenor what had happened and he figured that I hadn't released the emergency brake all the way and also went into high too soon. That was the closest thing to a driving lesson I've ever had in my life.

* * *

One of the few things on a car that the owner could fix himself—and often had to—were flats. Roads were rough and tires were of poor quality anyway. A patch kit and hand pump were standard equipment.

In 1917, my dad installed a compressor to run an air hammer for lettering monuments. Recognizing an opportunity when he saw one, Dad ran an extra line out to the street and let car owners inflate their tires—for a dime each. Until 1921, my dad's shop was the only place in town where you could air your tires. Then, Temple Hardware across the street put in a gasoline pump and their own air compressor and put up a sign that said FREE AIR. Dad's air business went flat fast.

One evening, when I was about fifteen, a fellow named Harry Stewart parked his Model T across the street from Dad's shop and called me over. One of his tires was going flat and he said

The Ford Psalm.

Some individual given over to space writing has written this very expressive Ford psalm, which the agent in these parts is expected to pay for at regular advertising rates: "The Ford is my auto; I shall not walk; it maketh me to lie under it in green pastures; it leadeth me into much trouble, it draweth on my purse, I go into the paths of death for it's sake, yea though I understand my Ford perfectly, I fear much evil, for the radius rod or the axle might break. It has a blowout in the presence of mine enemies; I anoint the tire with a patch; the radiator boils over. Surely this thing will not follow me all the days of my life, or I will dwell in the house of poverty forever."

Crawford County Democrat, July 30, 1914

that if I would fix it while he and his girlfriend were at the theater, he would give me a quarter—enough for a movie and popcorn. Recognizing a good deal when I heard one, I agreed.

Model T's had wooden spoke wheels with a steel rim fastened to the wheel with lugs. I jacked up the car, removed the lugs, took off the tire and rim, and laid them on the sidewalk. Standard tire-changing procedure was to walk around on the tire to break it loose from the rim, then use the tire tools to pry the tire off. When I removed the inner tube and ran my fingers around the inside of the tire, I found the small nail that had caused the puncture. I squeezed the tube, listening for the leak, and found a suspicious spot. I spit on it to see if it bubbled. It did.

In the patch kit was a small metal scratcher I used to rough up the tube around the leak. This cleaned the surface and also made a better seal when the patch was applied. I squeezed out some of the patch glue, smeared it around the hole, and blew on it for about a minute until it became sticky. (Some people preferred to ignite the glue with a match and let it burn for a couple of seconds to speed up this part of the process.) When the glue felt just right, I peeled the paper backing off the patch and pressed it over the hole.

I put the tube back into the tire, pumped it up, let the jack down, and put all the tools away. Changing Harry's tire had taken me the better part of an hour and I had been tired to begin with. Now I was worn out. At least I could relax until the show was out and collect my—

Spsssst . . . Maybe the patch didn't hold. Maybe it was a new leak. Whatever the cause, the same tire went flat again as I watched. I thought about Harry. I thought about my quarter. I thought about how tired I was. I thought about my quarter. I plodded home and went to bed.

About a week later I saw Harry Stewart again. He asked what had happened. I explained. Even though Harry had had to change his tire himself, he gave me my quarter anyway.

* * *

It was about 1919 before a mechanic by the name of Vandolah opened a garage on 4th Street. A year later, Ralph Bobbitt and his father started a Ford agency on 5th Street just east of the bank and installed the first gasoline pump in town. You put the end of the hose—no cutoff nozzle—into your car, and then you turned a crank that pumped the gasoline and registered from one to five gallons on a dial on the pump. There would always be gasoline left in the hose and you would have to lift it a couple of times to get all the gas out.

It wasn't long before someone invented the visible pump with a glass bowl that showed gallon markers. Now all you had to do was pump the bowl full and use the nozzle at the end of the hose to gravity out what you wanted. You still had to pay attention to see when your tank was full, but you didn't have to drain the hose.

Oil was sold by the quart, but not in cans. Near the pump would be a wire basket holding six or eight quart glass containers with screw-on pour spouts. Stations bought oil in bulk and refilled—and re-used—the glass containers. If a customer wanted to buy just the oil, he had to provide his own container.

Before leaving his home at Temple, a fellow named "Uncle Tommy" Cunningham changed the oil in his Nash coupe from a gallon jug he kept on a shelf in his garage at home. Before he had motored very far, the engine began making a strange, grinding noise. Then it started to smoke. By the time he got to Marengo—about four miles—foul-smelling clouds of black smoke were engulfing the car. He just barely made it to Jenner's garage.

The mechanic took one look at the engine and asked what on earth he had poured into it. In one awful moment Tommy remembered how unusually thick the motor oil had seemed when he poured it . . . and realized he had inadvertently picked up the gallon jug *setting next to the motor oil*—the jug of sorghum molasses.

Tommy put labels on his gallon jugs—and a new engine in his car.

* * *

By 1922, Bobbit's Agency had changed to selling Chevrolets and Dad bought a new Baby Grand touring car from him. One Sunday we went to the Providence Church's May meeting. Everyone brought food for a basket dinner. We had the only car there and of course people crowded around to look it over. When it was time for the services to start, Dad told me to stay with the car and watch our food.

I was sitting there behind the steering wheel, feeling very important, when a kid about ten years old walked up to the front of the car and put his face up against the radiator like he was trying to see inside it. A man standing nearby motioned for me to blow the horn, and I did. The boy exploded backwards from the car and was scared so bad he started to cry. I only had a few seconds to laugh before Dad appeared and I got a good chewing out.

That this community has not had serious automobile accidents is a puzzle to every prudent autoist. This community is as full of autos as a dog's hair is of fleas, and no more attention is given to the common courtesies of the road by some of them than if there were no such thing. They drive at reckless gaits, make pedestrians get off the crossings when the person on foot has the right of way by every moral and legal right, they turn every sort of caper in the streets, fail to give a reasonable share of the road and will run over you if you don't heed their honk. A halt should be called upon the reckless auto driving in this community, about the surest curing being a few stiff and steady fines.

The English News, September 8, 1916

At this time, there must have been a total of seven or eight automobiles in town. This article was actually written about the driving habits of Paddy Hughes, who tore around at speeds of twenty mph or more.

Of course . . .

Some things never change.

Boys riding horses fast when the streets are dusty should be arrested

Crawford County Democrat, July 21, 1891

The Great War

On election day, the first Tuesday in November, 1916, I was almost eight years old. Woodrow Wilson, who had been president for as long as I could remember, was running for his second term in a close race with an associate justice of the supreme court, Charles Evans Hughes. I hadn't given my support to either candidate, preferring to just enjoy the excitement of the rallys, the colorful posters and banners, and the constant debates among the adults. Most of Europe was at war and feelings about American involvement were running high. The Democrats were hoping to re-elect Wilson with the slogan "He kept us out of war."

That night, a big crowd gathered at the Luckett building to follow the election results. Jim Turley had built a new hardware store and had moved his merchandise out, leaving more space than was available at the opera house. In addition, the crowd could easily overflow onto Main Street, which it soon did. The restaurants and saloons stayed open, anticipating a late and profitable evening.

The election results came in by telegraph. Every few minutes, the operator at the depot would copy down the latest numbers on a slip of paper and hand it to one of the boys waiting at the counter. The young runner would then dash out the door, across the bridge, and up Main Street to the Luckett building, where the crowd would part, allowing him to rush in and hand the paper to John Luckett, who would then step up on a box and announce the results. Each time, one half or the other of the crowd would be pleased with the news and a loud and hopeful cheer would go up as the runner pressed his way back through the mass of onlookers to return to the depot. Being a runner was an exciting and important job and I wanted to do it at least once.

The main requirement for the job was not that you could run fast, but that you were tall enough to reach over the counter at the depot—and fight off the other boys who were eagerly waiting to make the next trip. I remember that my brother Clyde, who was ten, and Ted McMahel were there, along with two or three others. They were all more qualified—taller and bigger—than I was and I was never able to grab a slip and make the run. I followed Clyde a couple of times, but it just wasn't the same. I finally got tired and went home.

The election wasn't decided until early the next morning, when the California results came in. Wilson was elected to a second term and the Democrats—after getting a good night's sleep—celebrated the next evening by shooting anvils.

Shooting anvils is something revelers used to do to celebrate when they didn't have a cannon or dynamite handy. Here's how it's done: Find a thin metal rod about eight to ten feet long. Build a fire and leave one end of the rod in it. Borrow two anvils from local blacksmith shops. Set one anvil upright and pour a small amount of black powder on it, making a thin powder train off to one edge. Set the other anvil on top. Take the metal rod, one end of which should now be red hot, and touch it to the end of the powder train at the edge of the anvils. The resulting report will sound almost like a stick of dynamite—or a cannon.

The Democrats shot their anvils and celebrated until the early morning hours and again all the next day, relieved that we could now avoid the war in Europe.

A few months after the election, one day in April, my brother Claude picked up *The Louisville Times,* our only source of daily news from the outside world, which arrived about six o'clock each evening on the train. Dad would give one of us—usually me—a nickel to buy a copy and bring it home so he could read it after dinner. I don't remember why I didn't go that night, but I do remember Claude running into the house and holding up the front page with a headline that screamed: US DECLARES WAR ON GERMANY. Dad took the paper and we all gathered around as he read out loud.

I had missed my second chance at an important run from the depot.

* * *

What I remember most about World War I were the Liberty Loan Drives where they sold war bonds. At one bond drive, an army tank was unloaded from a railroad flatcar and driven through town. I remember it spinning around in the middle of Main Street, then climbing up on the edge of the sidewalk, which was about two feet higher than the street. People were amazed at what it could do. (The tank chipped a couple pieces of concrete off the sidewalk near my dad's shop and it remained that way for many years. Every time I noticed the chips, I thought of the tank.)

All the young men were in the service, so the older men made up a sort of police force for the home front called the Home

REAL TANK IN ACTION

A real bona fide battle tank made by Uncle Sam to vanquish the Hun; will be seen in

ENGLISH ON FRIDAY APRIL 25TH

This tank will be one of the features of the Victory Loan special train that will visit English. It weighs more than seven tons, is armored, about 16 feet long and 10 feet high. It will be carried on a special train and under its own power parade the streets of English. The special train will arrive at 7:00 a. m. and will leave at 1 p. m.

The Tank will be Manned by Soldiers who Have Seen Actual Service Overseas.

This advertisement contributed by L. A. Helmbrecht, I. M. Golden, S. C. Patton, N. E. Gobbel, H. Helshman, Sam Benz, J. E. Turley, Charles Moore, A. T. Turley, W. F. Sears, Moore & Hooten, T. L. Grimes, Bill Patton, Alson Roberts, Jesse E. Lessor.

The English News, April 18, 1919

Guard. I remember another war bond drive when there was a big crowd in town and the Home Guard marched up and down Main Street and did the manual of arms. The guard commander was a veteran of the Spanish-American War. He was dressed in his uniform and carried a sword. His little army looked about like the Minute Men at Bunker Hill must have looked. A few had canvas leggings, but no two uniforms were alike. Their rifles were all different makes and sizes. But, as far as I remember, they did a pretty good job of drilling.

They marched to the school grounds with a crowd following and at the school they laid their rifles on the ground about a foot apart and one man was left to guard them. He walked back and forth with a rifle on his shoulder. The guard was changed about every half hour.

I also remember a group of boys leaving for Camp Taylor, Kentucky. A railroad passenger car was on the siding by the milling company and the boys lined up beside the car and had their picture taken.

When the "War to End All Wars" ended, there was a big parade and celebration with everyone in town taking part.

A Ghost Story

When I was about eleven years old, my brother Clyde and I set some traps just north of our home, where there were some dens under a cliff. We ran our traps twice every day, before and after school. By the time school let out, there wasn't much daylight left and we had to rush to get to the traps and back before dark. The shortest distance to the cliffs was through the cemetery.

One evening we had run the traps and were returning. It was almost dark. As we started to climb over the fence into the cemetery, we heard something moaning and mumbling. We froze in our tracks and looked in the direction of the sound. In the semi-darkness we could see something black, moving over one of the graves. We were looking at each other, trying to decide what to do, when the moaning stopped.

Whatever was out there raised up and began moving in our direction. We dropped down and watched as it passed us and then turned toward town. After a few breathless moments, we stood up and followed.

When we got to the first street light, we could see that it was a woman dressed in black. Clyde ran past her to see who it was. She was a woman who lived in town whose mother had passed away. She had been kneeling down and praying over her mother's grave.

Horse Butter

About 1920, Nobel "Bobey" Smith asked my brother Claude, who was known as "Codger," to go with him to get a pound of country butter from "Aunt Sis" Standiford. She lived several miles out of town, so they decided to rent a couple of horses from Henry Perkins.

Most of Perk's horses were old and not worth much, but at least you could rent them cheap. Bobey and Codger paid a quarter each, saddled up, and were on their way. Bobey took along a half-gallon bucket for the butter.

On the way back, they started racing, running the old horses as fast as they could go. They pushed them just a little too hard.

Bobey's horse dropped dead in mid stride, fell in a heap—and smashed the bucket of butter flat.

Bobey wasn't hurt, but he was worried about what Perk would say and how much it would cost him to replace the horse. They took the bridle and saddle from the dead horse, agreed not to mention the racing part, and returned to Perk's barber shop. At a walk.

"Oh, don't worry about it. I was going to skin that old horse for his hide anyway." At that time, a horse hide was worth eight or ten dollars. Perk probably couldn't have sold the live horse for more than five.

Bobey was still the big loser. He lost his bucket and the butter.

Deephole and Highbanks

When I was a kid, a typical day included waiting for the morning train, riding with the drayman for an hour or so as he made his deliveries, then going swimming with my friends.

The local pulled in at about 8:30 A.M. and set a boxcar off on the siding with groceries and other items for delivery around town. Two or three of my friends and I would help the drayman, George Cummins, just to go along for the ride as he made his rounds. George didn't mind having us along, as we did a lot of the work.

After lunch we would head for one of two swimming holes. One, we called Deephole and the other, Highbanks. The shortcut to our swimming holes was through a farmer's cornfield, and, as kids will, not only had we beaten a path through his field, but we ran and chased each other and got into fights and, as a result, tore down some of his corn. He did a lot of complaining and threatened to get the law after us if we didn't stay out of his cornfield.

We didn't stay out of his field, but we did find ways not to advertise when we were going swimming. Before, we used to just go downtown and start yelling, "Let's go swimmin'!" Now, we would walk down the street looking for the other guys and, instead of yelling, we would make signs by holding up two fingers. Then we would congregate at the swimming holes.

One of the older boys who swam with us was Paddy Hughes. Paddy was always wetting someone's clothes and tying them in knots or throwing mud on someone who was almost dried off. We had worn curving paths along the muddy banks at both places so we could wet them and slide down into the water. One of Paddy's favorite pranks was to slip a sprig of greenbriars under the mud on one of the slides.

Most of us were his victims at one time or another, but the kid he picked on more than anyone else was Freddy Carmickle. One day Paddy showed up just as Freddy was drying off. He muddied him several times, tied his clothes in knots, and horse-laughed him until Freddy finally managed to get dressed and escape. Paddy then went for a swim, not knowing that Freddy had finally had enough.

Freddy went up the creek, found a heavy club, and came back to hide in the bushes and wait until Paddy finished his swim. While Paddy was drying off, Freddy slipped in behind him and hit him in the back of the head with the club. Paddy fell into the water and would have drowned if some of the other boys hadn't pulled him out. When he didn't come to right away, the boys carried him home. Paddy was unconscious for several hours. Word got out about what had happened and Freddy was put in jail.

When Paddy finally regained consciousness, he was told that Freddy was behind bars. Paddy admitted that it was all his fault and asked that Freddy be let out.

Fred Carmickle and Charles Hughes, aged 14 and 19 years respectively, became engaged in an altercation Thursday afternoon of last week while in swimming at the "High Banks," west of town, the Carmickle boy striking the Hughes boy on the head with a club, which is said weighed 8¾ pounds, knocking him unconscious, in which condition he remained for several hours. The Hughes boy was removed to his home where medical attention was rendered, and on Monday he was able to be up and is improving right along. The Carmickle boy was arrested by Marshal Loughmiller immediately after the occurrance, and placed in jail, but on Monday morning was released from custody. Boys, let's be more careful in our little "set-tos," someone is liable to be killed.

The English News, June 25, 1915

When Paddy recovered and got back on his feet, he and Freddy became good friends. And Paddy always seemed a little more mellow after that.

Farm for Sale

In March 1920, Dad put some farm acreage south of town up for sale. Shortly after the ad appeared, a man stopped at Dad's monument shop saying he was interested in seeing the farm. He apologized for the way he was dressed—dirty overalls and

FARM FOR SALE.

120 acres, good improvements, on state highway survey, 4 miles south of English, at a bargain. Alson Roberts, English.

The English News, March 23, 1920

an old work shirt—but he was in the area to deliver a steam engine and had just completed the installation. He owned a farm down in Gibson County and was looking to buy one up here. Since it was so late in the day, would it be all right if he stayed over and went to see the farm tomorrow? Of course, Dad offered to put him up overnight.

That evening at dinner, he told my brothers and me that he raised "cockytoots" on his farm (he called it a ranch) and he went on at great length about the care and feeding of these splendid—and valuable—birds.

Next day, he somehow had learned of another farmer also interested in perhaps buying a steam engine and would it be okay if he saw to that before going to the farm? This was the only nibble Dad had gotten so far, so . . .

That night after dinner he promised to send my brothers and me each a cockytoot as a present in return for our parents' kindness and hospitality. We all put in orders for our favorite color of plumage.

By the next day, the steam engine deal was almost finalized and he definitely could go and see the farm tomorrow. By the way, he was short of change and could Dad spare a dime for some chewing tobacco?

Dad finally told our fly-by-night cockytoot rancher to hit the road. Nothing was ever said about the sudden departure of our guest, but my brothers and I slowly figured out that the only exotic birds in our future were already in our hen house out back.

I don't remember who finally bought Dad's farm, but I do know that he never came to dinner.

Sunday Serenade

Sunday morning started out like any other morning in that there were the usual chores to do. We milked the cows and fed the chickens and hogs while Mother made breakfast.

About eight o'clock, the church bells would start ringing. They each had their own distinctive sound, and sometimes the first would be the farthest away, at Grantsburg, soon to be joined by the bells at Brownstown, Tunnel Hill, and Temple.

When the local Methodist and Presbyterian bells started, they replaced the distant bells, and combined in their own special, unique duet until they were drowned out by the first bell at the Christian Church, which was just down the hill. This was Dad's cue to announce that it was time to get ready for Sunday School.

Dad taught Sunday School for years and, as Mother got everyone dressed, he would go over his lessons. When we were all shined and polished, Dad would snap open his change purse and give each of us a few pennies for the collection plate. Mom almost never went to Sunday School with us, although she always went to the evening service with Dad. Looking back, I guess that hour or so on Sunday morning was the only time she had to herself all week.

Going Modern

My dad worked with the same tools and techniques that craftsmen had used to sculpt marble and granite for thousands of years—one hammer, one chisel, and one chip of stone at a time. Finishing the lettering and decorative work on one monument took him the better part of a week.

He bought a pneumatic air hammer in 1917, and his weekly output tripled. By 1923, sand blasters were available and Dad could start laying out the design in the morning and have the stone completely finished by noon.

The tools and techniques for home-owning hadn't changed much either. Even though our home was only a couple of blocks from the center of town, it was almost like living on a farm. We had thirteen acres of hilly pasture for a pair of milk cows, some chickens, hogs, tame rabbits, a couple of dogs, and four or five cats. And no electricity or indoor plumbing. If we left town—which was seldom—Dad rented a horse and surrey from the livery stable.

We had our first brush with the modern age in 1916, when Dad bought a new Overland motorcar. The only road that went more than a mile out of town was the pike to Grantsburg, but that was perfect for an evening's outing.

Our water supply came from an underground cistern, which was filled by rain water flowing off the roof and through a metal box filled with charcoal. Whenever it rained, Dad would wait a few minutes for the roof to wash clean, then go outside and turn a valve that directed the water into the cistern.

This arrangement was very handy. If we needed water, we just stepped out the kitchen door, turned a crank, and filled a bucket. And there was always a bucket of water in the kitchen with a dipper that we all used whenever we wanted a drink. For a bath, we drew a bucket or two, heated them on the wood stove, and poured them into the wash tub—which we had dragged into a bedroom. In the summer, I usually washed every day in the creek. In the winter, baths were a lot less frequent.

In about 1918 we had a sink installed in the kitchen with a pitcher pump next to it. This was *really* handy. Now that we could pump our drink of water directly from the cistern, the bucket and dipper disappeared. If, however, the pump sat too long without being used, it would "lose its prime" and a cup of water was always left handy to pour down into the pump and get it going again.

Around 1920 we got our first electric light. I remember a man came and bored a hole through the wall, ran wires in, and fastened them up the wall through a switch and across the ceiling. There was a wide opening between the living and dining rooms and Dad had him hang the bulb so it would light up both rooms. I could hardly wait for it to get dark. I can still remember our whole family talking about how much more light it made than the coal-oil lamps we had used for so long. It was easier, too. Every day or two the lamps had to be filled, the wicks had to be trimmed so the flame would burn evenly, and the flues had to be cleaned.

In 1925 Dad remodeled the whole house and added a second story. We got city water, added an indoor bathroom, and even had cold—and hot—running water at the kitchen sink. We didn't get rid of the outside toilet, though; we just didn't use it as much.

The next year we added central heating, a hot water system called an Arcola. We still had to carry in coal, but now we just fired up one unit and the whole house stayed comfortable.

In the winter of 1928, Dad was sick and never got out when the weather was bad. He bought a radio and was soon staying home to hear his favorite programs—regardless of the weather.

We didn't have mechanized refrigeration, but that wasn't really inconvenient since ice was delivered right to the house. And we usually had a fire going in the wood stove in the kitchen most of the time anyway—which I wasn't responsible for.

As far as I was concerned, the Modern Age had arrived.

A Woman's Touch

My brother Junior was born on December 9, 1920. Mother was forty-two years old and he was her sixth child. It was a difficult birth and her health was never the same again. She was weak at best and, more often than not, sick in bed.

In June of 1922, Dad took her on the train to the Deaconess Hospital in Louisville, where she had surgery. When she came home, she was bedfast. Since Coy was working, Codger was studying to be a teacher, and Clyde was helping Dad at the shop, it fell to me to stay home and look after Mother—and Helen and Junior—during the day. That was a miserable summer for me, not only because I was used to being outside with the other kids but also because Mother often didn't know where she was or who I was. She gained some strength, but that almost made it worse, since she would get up and wander off if I didn't watch her.

My mother died on September 20, 1922. Coy was twenty, Codger was eighteen, Clyde was fifteen, Helen was seven, and Junior, who Mother never really knew, was twenty-two months. It seemed like the end of the world, and I remember feeling guilty that I had resented being stuck at home with her instead of out playing. I wished she could just be home again, even if she didn't know me. I desperately wanted to hold her hand one more time. Her passing left a big hole in all our lives, but at thirteen, I probably needed her most.

Shortly after Mother's death, Coy joined the Navy, and Codger got a job teaching in Montana. Clyde was still working at the monument shop, so it was still up to me to take care of Helen and Junior. For a while, Dad did the cooking when he came home from work. We always had chickens, and I would occasionally dress one so that when he came home we would have a fry.

That Christmas, Santa left a toy train for Junior and me. I was thrilled and was afraid to let him touch it for fear he would damage it. I made a deal with him—I would make tunnels out of cardboard and do all the engineering, and he could do all the watching. We both got a lot of entertainment out of that train.

Living without a woman's touch soon got old to all of us left at home, so Dad hired an elderly lady named Mrs. King to do the cooking and housekeeping. She stayed about a year, then Dad hired a Mrs. Patton, who helped out until Dad remarried in 1924. His new wife was Fern Benham. She moved in with her twelve-year-old son from a previous marriage and it began to feel like we were a family again. I was almost sixteen and taking care of myself, but she was a good, religious woman and made a fine mother for Helen and Junior.

Dad had a second family by Fern—two girls, Eleanor and Maxine, and another boy, Linden.

The Hidden Fountain

In the early 1890s, a Dr. Hazelwood built a hotel on the property just south of James Sloan's. It was a two-story frame building with large porches both upstairs and down for the guests to lounge on. There was a saloon about one hundred feet from the hotel, connected by two tall picket fences about six feet apart. (This was so people traveling from the hotel to the saloon and back couldn't be seen.)

The hotel was called the Hazelwood Springs Hotel because it boasted flowing sulfur springs. In those days, mineral baths had a great health value.

In front of the hotel was a round stone basin about sixteen

feet in diameter and about eight feet deep. Steps led down to the bottom, where there were three flowing wells. Each well had a Bedford stone ring on top where the water overflowed.

The Hazlewood Springs Hotel burned after only a few years of operation. The stone basin was filled in and a dwelling was built where the hotel had been.

* * *

Twenty years later, a man named George Stewart purchased the property. He heard about the buried basin and managed to locate it. I remember watching them clean the black mud out. They even got the sulfur wells flowing again.

Stewart kept the basin and sulfur wells open for about two years, but when the creek flooded it would back up into the basin and leave a deposit of mud. It was a problem to keep clean, so Stewart filled it in again.

The stone basin from the Hazlewood Springs Hotel is still there, but it would be hard to find.

Airplanes

The first time I saw an airplane on the ground was at the Crawford County Fair in Marengo. It was about 1923 and they had advertised that an airplane would fly in from Louisville and land on Thursday at 10:00 A.M. There was a big crowd waiting and watching the eastern sky. It was a gray, overcast day, but finally, someone with sharp eyes yelled "There it comes!" The fair officials had a hard time holding the crowd back so the plane would have room to land.

There were two men flying the plane, and when it landed and rolled up toward us, one of them jumped out and grabbed one of the wings. He turned the plane to keep it from hitting the bandstand.

Shortly after the plane landed, it started to rain. The crowd paid no attention and swarmed around the plane to get a closer look and see what it felt like. Well, not everyone in the crowd ignored the rain. I remember getting under one of the wings for protection.

The field at the fairground wasn't too long, so when the plane got ready to take off that afternoon, the pilot had three or four men to hold it until he got the motor revved up. He gave the signal to turn loose and everyone held their breaths until the plane cleared the fairground fence.

* * *

About four years later, someone reported that an airplane with engine trouble had made a forced landing on Perry Kimble's farm at the north edge of town. Within a half hour a big crowd had gathered.

It turned out that the pilot was a barnstormer who had landed to take up passengers. The field was a little small and it was late in the afternoon, so he decided to relocate to another field about a mile north and told everyone to come back in the morning.

Some of us went to the new field to watch him land. There was a small ditch hidden in the field and he hit it when he came in. The plane tipped up and broke both ends off the propeller. The pilot wasn't injured, so we took him to the nearest phone and he called his home field at Vincennes. I kept one end of the broken propeller as a souvenir.

The next morning, someone showed up in a Model T Ford coupe with a new propeller tied on top. It was quickly installed and he had a big weekend taking up passengers for three dollars each or two for five dollars.

Two of his five-dollar passengers were Howard Eastridge and me. We both squeezed into the passenger seat in front of the pilot, and I still remember my excitement when the bumpy take-off suddenly smoothed out as we became airborne. The pilot usually made two or three large circles to about fifteen hundred

Fly Over The

English Reunion

Next Week = August 1, 2, 3, 4

Watch!! for FREE RIDE TICKETS Dropped Over Your Town Wednesday, August 1, Next Week!!!

Will Carry Passengers at the Reunion Thursday, Friday and Saturday. $3 for One, $2.50 Each for Two Passengers.

Landing Field 1 Mile East of English on the Lafe Grant Farm

Stunt Flying Over Grounds

Boxing Wednesday Night

Howard McLain, New Albany, and Willie Peck, Corbin, Ky., will meet in the 10-round main go. Battle Royal, two 6-round bouts and two 4-round bouts in the preliminaries. Seats now on sale at the Democrat Office, English.

3 Rides, Amusements, *and* Dancing

Admission and Parking Space Free

At William H. English Park

ENGLISH, IND.

Crawford County Democrat, July 26, 1928

or two thousand feet, then descended the same way. It was a thrill to see English from the air.

But Howard and I wanted more. We figured we would impress the pilot with our knowledge of airplane jargon and we asked if he would do a "loop-the-loop." He just smiled . . . and obliged.

Being upside-down in an open-seat airplane at fifteen hundred feet without a seat belt is one of my—and my stomach's—more memorable experiences. Howard and I were both very quiet the rest of the way down. The pilot was still smiling when we got out.

I carved the date on the broken prop. It was November 26, 1927.

Spelunkers I

About 1921, my father was part owner of a coal mine near Mifflin. The miner who worked the mine would come to English occasionally to see Dad and he usually wore his miner's cap, which had a square piece of metal on the front where the light hooked on. The light had a compartment that unscrewed and held a few lumps of carbide. Above that was a container that held water. A valve between them allowed water to drop on the carbide, making gas, which was lit by a flint striker. It made a bright light and my brother Clyde and I talked Dad into getting us each one. When we wore them downtown at night, you could see us coming from far away. It wasn't long until other kids got them and we all brightened up the whole town.

One of my favorite places to explore during the summer was Toney Cave, so-called because it was located on John Toney's farm. (Today, the entrance is not far from Highway 64. Back then it was quite a hike out into the country to get there.) The first thing we did when we got our miner's lights was to go into Toney Cave to try them out.

When you first enter Toney Cave, there's a long slide down to the main room, where there are lots of initials written in candle smoke on the cave ceiling. Several passages lead off in different directions. One place is so narrow, you have to work your way sideways to get through. We called it Fatman's Misery. Another passage leads up a slope and through a narrow room we called The Upstairs. In another direction is the only rock formation in the cave (at least that we ever found), a stalagmite we called Glass Rock.

Another passage has an opening so small you can only peep through and see as far as your lights will reach. This is known as The Keyhole. One boy told a story about squeezing through The Keyhole and coming out at Gilliland's spring, a half mile away. Of course, no one believed him.

One day when Guido Patton and I were returning from the cave, we heard someone crying. We found a little boy standing by a tree sobbing. He had followed some older boys who were headed for the cave, but he became frightened, turned back, and got lost in the woods. We felt like heroes when we rescued him.

The Donkey

When my father was part owner of the coal mine near Mifflin, the miners used a donkey to pull the heavy coal carts. When the mine closed down, we got the donkey. His name was Old Jack. All we had was a bridle, but we rode him quite often.

One afternoon I was riding on a county pike north of town when a Model T Ford passed me with the top down and I noticed a couple of girls in the back seat. I wanted to show off and decided to try and keep up. I started whipping Old Jack and we were staying right behind the car. The girls were looking back and laughing and watching the donkey cowboy.

Now Jack was a cantankerous old cuss and at times would balk if you got to pushing him too hard. This was one of those times. All at once he decided he had had enough. He put his front feet out and his head down and he came to a screeching stop. I sailed over his head and skidded down the hard pike on my back. And my front. And my sides.

The Model T stopped, backed up, and the driver asked if I was hurt. I was, but I was more embarrassed, so I told him no. He drove away and I led Jack to a nearby spring. I was skinned from my head to my knees. I washed off the blood and sat there for about an hour before I was able to make it back home. I led Jack all the way.

* * *

My brother Clyde was riding Jack in the west end of town one night and passed a house where several young girls were having a birthday party. Clyde rode Jack up to an open kitchen window where they were eating ice cream and cake. When Jack poked his head through the window, the girls turned over their chairs and ran from the room, screaming.

Clyde and Old Jack rode off into the night.

The Shack

At some time in their young lives, most boys feel the need for a tree house or a headquarters of some kind. Most of the pasture behind my house was hilly, with one particularly high spot my friends and I called English Hill. We decided to build ourselves a shack there so we could have a good view of the town. We could see all the way up Fifth Street, all over the west end, and all the way to the courthouse.

It took quite a while and a lot of hard work. We picked up discarded boards, roofing materials, and whatever else from all over town. We even found an old cast-iron stove and somehow manhandled it up to the location. When we finally had our materials, we cut some posts from trees in the woods, set them in the ground, and started nailing on boards.

We had metal roofing and ran the stovepipe straight through with an elbow at the top end to turn away from the wind so the stove would have a good draft. We made a door, but no windows (so much for the view). The cracks between the boards let in enough light to see pretty good. We were usually there three or four days every week.

One cold day that winter, Zenor "Jug" Brown and I arrived at the shack and found my brother Clyde, Ted McMahel, and Fred Johnson already there. They had a fire going, but had fastened the door. The wind was sharp and we were getting cold. No matter what we said, they wouldn't let us in. I knew that Jug had some .38 caliber cartridges in his pocket (no big deal at the time), so I took some and climbed up on the roof. I dropped several of them down the smokestack, which went directly into the stove.

The shells started exploding. The stove door blew open, and the shack was filled with smoke before they could unfasten the door and escape. They came out coughing, fanning, and swearing, but otherwise unhurt. When the smoke cleared, we all went back inside and it was business as usual.

* * *

Around 1921, the Ku Klux Klan was active in Indiana and it was probably some local members who were responsible for burning a cross on the hill near our shack. It was an ideal location, since it could be seen from all over town, but we felt like they had trespassed on our property and should be taught a lesson. We decided to show them up by doing a better job of cross-burning than they had. We went into the woods, cut two poles, wired them together, wrapped the whole thing with burlap, and ended up with a twenty-foot-high cross, at least half again as large as theirs.

Since we wanted to do a first-class job, we needed dynamite to set off and attract attention. One of the guys spoke up and said he knew where to get some. The next day he showed up with several sticks of dynamite, a box of caps, and a roll of fuse. We didn't ask where they came from, even though we all knew that a local contractor kept his supplies in a barn across from the jail—where our friend's father was sheriff.

We dug a hole to set up the cross and cut stakes to drive in the ground to hold the dynamite. (Dynamite exploded a foot or so off the ground will make the sound carry much farther.) After dark we carried the cross from where we had hidden it in the woods, soaked it good with kerosene, and set it up. We tied the dynamite on the stakes and cut the fuses into different lengths so the explosions would go off in roughly 15-second intervals. By the time we got everything ready, it was almost nine o'clock.

One boy went to each stick of dynamite and another lit the cross. About the time the cross was in full flame, we lit the fuses and ran back out of the way. The dynamite started going off and the whole hill was lit up.

We were enjoying the show when we saw several men coming up the hill—probably some of the original cross-burners. We didn't wait around to find out. By the time they reached the top, we had disappeared into the woods.

* * *

We had used all the dynamite, but there were a lot of caps and fuse left, so we hid them. Occasionally we'd shoot some of the caps. (We didn't realize how dangerous they were.) The routine was to cut a six-inch fuse, put it in the cap, light it, and throw it over the hill. We'd fire off several, and return the rest to the shack.

One day Jug Brown came to the shack and took the caps and

fuse home with him. Behind his house was a creek, and across the creek was a field. He started in the field, blowing up pumpkins. Then he started throwing caps in the creek and making water spouts. He had more caps than he had fuse, so the fuses began to get shorter and shorter. Soon the fuses were down to about an inch, just barely long enough to light and throw before the cap exploded.

Jug was holding a cap in his left hand and using his right hand to light the fuse. He struck a match and touched it to the fuse just as the match went out. The fuse was lit, but he didn't know it. As he reached for another match, the cap went off in his hand.

Jug told me that when he looked at his hand, he saw the bones sticking out where his thumb and two fingers had been. Little sprays of blood were coming out all around them. He ran past his house, shouted to his mother, and kept going to the doctor's office, which was about a block away.

Jug lost the thumb and two fingers on his left hand, but he gained a new nickname. For the rest of his life, Jug Brown was known as "Thumbless Jug."

Bloomer Boy

> **The Star Bloomer Girls, a traveling aggregation of lady ball players, will cross bats with the English nine on the local diamond Friday, May 21, 1915. They travel in a special car, and no doubt will give our boys a good stiff game.**

The English News, May 14, 1915

The Bloomer Girls traveled around the country playing small-town teams like ours. They had a pretty good team, but a weak pitcher. After playing English, they hired one of our pitchers, Edgar Longest, to go along with them for the rest of the season—dressing him in bloomers and calling him "Liz." From then on, the hometown boys also called him Liz.

The game of ball between the Bloomer Girls and the English team on the local diamond last Friday afternoon, resulted in a score of 7 to 8 in favor of the home team. It was the first bump the Girls had received since leaving headquarters at Indianapolis on Sunday before, and they, as well as a great many of our people, were surprised at the game put up by our team.

Nicknames

When I was a boy it seemed 'most everyone somehow picked up a nickname. Usually, it stayed with them from then on.

My oldest brother, Coy, once told a big story about running onto a bear in the woods and killing it. He was given the name "Bearkiller." My brother Claude, named after our uncle, was always called "Codger."

Another brother, Clyde, was a boxer in the mid 1920s. At that time there was a popular comedian named Clyde Cook. My brother became known as "Cook" Roberts.

My brother Linden—who already had the nickname "Bob"

even as a small boy—was a pretty rough talker. One time we had the preacher over for dinner. Everything had gone well until dessert. Bob grabbed the pitcher to pour cream on his strawberries and spilled some. His mother took the pitcher away from him and poured the cream herself. This made Bob mad, so he grabbed the sugar bowl and announced in a loud voice: "I'll put the damned sugar on!" To this day, some still call him "Strawberry."

When my cousin Glen was a small boy, his older brother was fitted for glasses. Glen thought they made his brother look very dignified and wanted a pair for himself. For several days he went around squinting, trying to convince his parents that he, too, was nearsighted. He didn't get the glasses, but he was forever after known as "Squint."

Guy Longest was an only child and his mother kept him spotlessly clean. His nickname was "Dirty." Arnie Longest was known as "Slick."

A fat boy named Harry Temple acquired the name "Tub." His brother, John, had a problem with his face twitching and his eyes blinking. He was called "Blinkey." Fred Temple, for reasons unknown, was "Tootsie."

Wayne Gregory was well-read and thought he was a little smarter than the other boys. Everyone called him "Pinhead." Some of the other boys in the Gregory family were "Pluto," John "Horse," "Clubfoot," "Softy," "Shimdig," "Kastey," and "Dolly" (Herbert).

Harold Conn was at the English Reunion years ago when brick ice cream first hit the market. At that time, it was called Hokie-Pokie Ice Cream. He ate so much it made him sick. From then on, he carried the name "Hokie."

Fred Mathers worked at a mental hospital in Indianapolis. About his third day on the job, one of the inmates hit him on the head with a heavy teacup. Fred quit his job, made the mistake of telling the story, and became known as "Teacup" Mathers.

Forrest Hudson lived on Little Blue River and came to school one morning with a story about a huge catfish he had caught. To this day, he is known as "Catfish" Hudson.

Raymond Spears had a talent for telling tall tales with a straight face. Everyone called him "Windy." One afternoon in the 1930s, Windy came running down Main Street in a big hurry. "Hey, Windy," someone said, "tell us a big one." "I ain't got time," Windy said. "A train just hit a car at the Temple crossing." And with that, he jumped into his truck and sped away. Word spread fast about the wreck and people were soon on their way to the Temple crossing about three miles east of town (myself included). All we found at the crossing was a traffic jam of suckers who had been taken in by Windy. He laughed about that one for years.

Walter Asher got into a fight with another boy near a filling station where the owner had set out some shade trees which were about four feet high. Walter uprooted one of the trees and used it to fight with. And that's how "Shadetree" Asher got his name.

Russell Pro was called "Cocky" because he thought he was a little bit above the other boys and was always turning his nose up at everything. When he was about eighteen, he won a big box of candy on a punchboard at Jesse Leasor's store and said he would pick it up that night to take to his girlfriend. Jesse didn't think much of Cocky and decided to get him in trouble. He carefully opened the box, removed the candy, and refilled it with rocks and horse manure (both of which were plentiful in the streets).

About dark, Cocky picked up the candy and headed off to see his girlfriend. Fortunately—or unfortunately, depending on your point of view—Jesse had added a few too many rocks. Cocky became suspicious and opened the box before he got to his girl's house. The girlfriend didn't get the candy and Cocky probably avoided getting a new nickname.

Zenor Brown's nickname was "Jug," but after he blew off his thumb and two fingers with a blasting cap, he was called "Thumbless Jug." His father, Lee, was known as "Big Jug" and his younger brother, Lovell, was "Little Jug."

Clarence Austin was "Big Hooley" and his brother, Glen, was "Little Hooley."

Raymond and Arley Sarles were "Cricket" and "Crooked

Mouth." Floyd and William Patton were "Chigger" and "Soaker Bill." Charles and Clifford Brown were "Pekey" and "Buss." Felix and Russell Hammond were "Briggs" and "Nub."

Nova Gobbel went to Purdue and was known as "Turk" because of his last name, but everyone in English knew him as "Pooch."

Some of my other favorite nicknames are "Dry Bones" Ott, "Derby" Smith, "Frosty" Jones, "Chalky" Miller, "Bunk" McMahel, "Boone" Harmon, "Tater Top" Morris, "Pickaxe" Toney, "Riggle" Blevins, and "Chank" Dodd.

My name is Everett, but I've been called "Ebb" as far back as I can remember. Several years ago, the Crawford County Security Company mailed me a letter addressed to "Everett Roberts." The Postmaster returned it, stamped "Addressee Unknown."

The Petrified Body

In 1897 a woman who lived on Court Hill buried her deceased sister in her back yard (perfectly legal at that time). When she sold the house, in about 1921, it was agreed she would have the body reinterred in the English Cemetery.

The casket turned out to be metal, with a plate glass top. The young woman clearly visible inside was wearing a black dress with a white lace collar and cuffs. Her dark hair, eye lashes, face, and hands were perfect. She could have been dead only a few hours, instead of over a quarter of a century.

Word spread fast, and by the time the coffin had been moved to the cemetery, a crowd had gathered. More people began to arrive, so the burial was delayed until evening so everyone could view the phenomenon.

It was said that the casket had been submerged in lime water and that was why the body was in such good condition. She was finally reburied and that was that. Except . . .

Two local businessmen couldn't forget how much interest had been generated by this novelty. It was clear that every person there would have gladly paid for the privilege to view a quarter-century-old, perfectly preserved body. And if the lime water had petrified it, then it would look the same indefinitely, allowing even more people to see it.

Within a month, arrangements had been made to re-exhume the body and examine it to see if it was petrified. Most of the same crowd was back again, including myself. The casket was hauled out and placed on two sawhorses. Dr. Fred Gobbel, the local doctor, and Dr. Johnson from Milltown were there to make the examination.

The workers who dug up the casket couldn't get it open, so the decision was made to break the plate glass. The doctors probed the body and declared it to be waxlike, but hardly petrified. Maybe in a few hundred years . . .

She was re-re-buried by placing the metal casket in a wooden one. And the local entrepreneurs went back to being local businessmen.

Going Places

Owning an automobile in the early days was definitely a status symbol, but there were drawbacks, too. For one, the infernal machines didn't work half the time. When they did, there wasn't any place to drive them.

About 1910, the county built several roads going out of town,

English will double her trade if we get better roads. Every hill road leading to this place should be piked.

Crawford County Democrat, May 4, 1899

a mile each in different directions. Because of the spindly legs they gave the town on a map, they were called spider pikes. About 1914, the pike going south was extended to Grantsburg—about four miles—and the people who had cars would make a nice evening's drive there and back.

The spider pike going east ended abruptly two miles short of Temple and the only road was also the creek bed. No one motored to Temple for an evening's drive.

Going north and west was more of the same. The pike ended at the Dog Creek bridge, which crossed the creek, but the creek then became the only road. Brownstown was accessible by more creek than pike.

If you really *had* to go north, to Paoli for example, you would begin by going south, to Curby, then east and north to Marengo, winding through Valeen and eventually to Paoli. A round trip like this would take the better part of a day.

Times were booming in 1924, and the state was building a major north/south thoroughfare that would go right through town. This was as momentous as the arrival of the railroad. English would soon be a major business hub!

I remember when the first road-building machinery arrived. It was a steam shovel shipped in by rail and I watched as they fired it up and unloaded it from a flatcar. It had an upright boiler and burned coal. A Longest boy nicknamed "Elmpeeler" was the fireman and the operator was called Ringo. The shovel was followed by quite a few onlookers as it lumbered up Main Street to the north edge of town and started digging. It had huge teeth and everyone was amazed at how fast it could fill a wagon.

Several farmers hired on as drivers to haul dirt. A man with a team of horses could make five dollars a day—a lot more than he could make farming. When the wagon was full, all the driver had to do to empty it was pull a lever and the bottom would open up and dump the whole load. There was a crank on the side that closed the bottom and the wagon was ready to be refilled.

For several days, while the shovel was near town, there was always a crowd of sightseers who came just to watch it work. I played hooky from school to watch. It didn't occur to me at the time, but I was there, after more than a hundred years, when Main Street finally arrived at James Sloan's cabin.

* * *

The next summer, I got a job working on the road. As I recall, the wage for a laborer was twenty-five cents per hour—about two dollars a day. I heard that a hard worker laying bedrock could make four or five dollars a day, so I got a job laying bedrock.

The bedrock was broken up at the quarry into foot-thick pieces, hauled to the work site, and dumped onto the graded road. My job—we worked in two-man teams—was to hand-set each piece on edge and work small pieces called spalls in between the larger pieces. The grade was sixteen feet wide, and for every foot we moved forward, we each earned a dime. It was a tough, backbreaking job, but I was sixteen, in good shape, and I didn't mind hard work—especially when it paid up to five dollars a day.

By noon I was getting pretty hungry. I had been told not to bring my lunch because everyone ate at a boardinghouse nearby that was run by a woman named Teaford. She charged a quarter per meal—not bad for all you could eat—and you paid at the end of the week. When the lunch whistle blew, I was definitely ready for some good food and plenty of it.

As we filed into the dining room, I guess I was the only new face and Mrs. Teaford took me aside. She said I would have to pay in advance. I didn't have a quarter and she wouldn't let me into the dining room. I went back outside.

I was hungry as a bear and knew I couldn't put in an afternoon in the hot sun laying bedrock on an empty stomach. And, since the road was mostly closed, I couldn't expect to get a ride if I started walking the ten miles back to town. What to do?

I started walking. Luckily, within a few miles I got a ride with a clothing salesman making his rounds and got home for a good meal.

About a week later, I hired on with the road crew again, but this time I brought my dinner bucket. The closest I got to bedrock this time was loading it onto trucks at the quarry. The job I liked best was building shoulders along the edge of the road with a shovel.

* * *

State Road 37 was completed in 1925. In July of 1926, the first stop signs in town—a total of five—were installed at all intersections with the new highway. Motorists stopped, but didn't realize they also had to yield the right-of-way to the traffic on Main Street. The marshal sat downtown and stopped violators for a couple of weeks, not to ticket them, but to instruct them in the use of the new signs.

* * *

Now that Paoli was suddenly only seventeen miles away, some of the younger drivers started bragging about making the trip in twenty minutes or less. In 1928, Nova Gobbel had a new Nash sedan and he invited some of us to go with him to Paoli. As we left downtown, he asked us to time the trip. He kept the steering wheel in one hand and a bottle of Coca-Cola in the other as we slipped and skidded along the gravel-covered hills and curves. We never saw another car—fortunately—the whole time. The seventeen-mile trip took eighteen minutes.

That was typical of the amount of traffic back then. Perry "Buzzard" Starr, who lived about two miles north of town, told me that one winter after a two-inch snowfall, he didn't see a tire track on the State Road for three days.

Big Business

In about 1925, I was working part-time at the milling company and part-time for my dad at his monument shop. Our chicken house at home wasn't in use, so I decided to raise a few chickens. I figured I could raise a hundred pullets and clear about fifty dollars.

I went to Turley's Hardware and bought a small kerosene heater for about six dollars, a sheet of galvanized metal to make a hover, and a feeder. I fixed a floor in the chicken house and bought a hundred baby chicks for ten cents each. By this time I had about thirty-two dollars invested in the project, not including my work and the kerosene and feed.

When the chicks were about a week old, I was painting in the house and went out to fill the kerosene heater and fire it up. I should have stayed with it for a few minutes and turned it down, but I was in a hurry to get back to my painting. About fifteen minutes later, our neighbor, Oscar Longest, was banging on the back door, telling me my chicken house was on fire. Everything burned up—chicks and equipment. That was the end of my chicken business.

We also had a hog pen that wasn't in use, and one day Zenor Brown asked me if I'd like to buy a weaned pig for a dollar. Seeing as how I already had a pen to put it in, I thought that sounded like a good deal, especially since I was still working at the mill where I could get the sweepings off the floor—cracked corn, wheat, bran—for nothing. Choice feed for a pig. This time there was no way I could go wrong.

The next day Zenor showed up with a sack (a pig in a poke). When I dumped my pig out of the sack, I noticed it seemed awfully small for a weaned pig, but I wasn't too worried since I could give it all kinds of choice feed.

A month later it had only gained about five pounds when it should have gained at least thirty. Its body hadn't gotten any bigger, just its legs and ears were longer and its hair stood straight out like a porcupine. Not only was it ugly, but it was so small it kept getting out of the pen and I had to chase it all over the yard to catch it.

One day it got out and I just ignored it. It rooted and squealed around in the yard awhile, then disappeared into the woods. That was the end of my hog business.

A fellow named Tommy Thompson traded me six rabbits and their hutch for a 410 double-barreled shotgun. I wasn't in the rabbit business very long before I had seventy-five of them and I had to tear down an old corn crib and use the lumber to enlarge their hutch. I was selling them for breeding stock and meat, but they were multiplying faster than I could find a market. I shut down the production line and went out of the rabbit business.

Sometime later, Zenor Brown (yes, *that* Zenor Brown) told me about a farmer who had an old mule to die and had dragged it out into the woods and left it for the varmints. Zenor figured we could skin the mule in half a day and get ten dollars for the hide—five dollars apiece—which was pretty good wages. I must have forgiven Zenor for the pig by then, because I agreed to go. We got our knives sharpened and hitched a ride out to the farm, about two miles south of town.

We went into the woods and found the mule. He was already smelling pretty rank, even though it was March and the weather had been cool.

"How long did you say this mule has been dead?" I asked.

"Only about a week." Zenor noticed the look of disgust on my face. "Maybe a little longer."

Well, we had come all this way—and I could use the money . . .

Two hours later we had one side skinned. When we turned the mule over, the smell got a lot worse. We could see its ribs through a rotted-out place in its side. I decided to quit right there and start back, but Zenor wouldn't give up.

"The job's already half done. And we can cut around the rotted part. Of course, if you don't want the five dollars . . . "

Two hours after that we finally finished, put the hide in a burlap sack, and dragged it back to the highway. Henry Smith came along in the milling company truck. We threw the hide in the back and got into the cab with Henry.

"Where in the world have you fellows been?"

"Skinning a mule."

"Roll the window down and let some fresh air in!"

Henry let us out at the poultry house, more than glad to get rid of us. The poultry man dumped the mule hide out onto the floor. His nose wrinkled.

"How long has that animal been dead?"

"I don't know," Zenor said. "Not too long."

The poultry man spread the hide out on the floor. He sprinkled about a gallon of salt on it and then gave us three dollars each. I decided there must be easier ways of making money.

And that was the end of my career as a mule skinner.

The Boom Before The Bust

English's finest decade was probably during the Roaring Twenties. With the new state road coming through town, business was booming. People came for miles to hire on at one of the four factories. Others who had moved away to find work came back home to find jobs. The population soared to almost a thousand.

Around this time, there were nine or ten grocery stores, three restaurants, two drugstores, a theater, a bowling alley, two hardware stores, a skating rink, a dance hall, two garages, four filling stations, a ten-cent store, three clothing stores, two hotels, two boardinghouses, three barbershops, four doctors, two dentists, five or six lawyers, and several bootleggers. All were doing well, and there wasn't an empty house in town.

One of the employers in town was the canning factory, which had been operating as far back as I could remember. It was started by a group of English businessmen and, in season (July through September), employed about a hundred people. It was later sold to Ed Griggs, of Edwardsville, who operated it until about 1928.

The basket factory was organized by William Rice of Louisville. He sold stock and began operating in 1921. It was known as the Rice Basket and Box Company.

The Car Shops was opened in about 1925 by Grover Stokes, who was from Chicago. Stokes built railroad refrigerator cars and at one time employed about 150 men. They turned out one refrigerator car each day.

The Turley Hub and Rim Company started operating in about 1924. They made wagon hubs and rims for the Huntingburg Wagon Works and also made a farm wagon called the English Wagon.

I worked at three of these plants. In about 1926, Ed Griggs hired two other boys and me to get the canning factory cleaned up and ready to open. He was paying twenty cents per hour. One of the boys working with me was Edison Roberson. He asked Griggs for a raise to twenty-five cents. Griggs said no.

While we were unloading a carload of cans, Griggs left to go uptown. Edison tried to get me and the other boy to go on strike. I was satisfied with twenty cents an hour, but Edison convinced the other boy to go along. They sat down on the track nearby and waited. A half-hour later, Griggs came back and asked the boys what they were doing. "We are striking for higher wages," they said. Griggs was not impressed. "Get back to work, or you are fired." They jumped up immediately and started unloading cans. That was probably English's first—and shortest—strike.

I worked at the basket factory for about a year. The pay was ten cents an hour for a ten-hour day, six days a week. We were paid twelve dollars every two weeks—no taxes, social security, or withholding.

In 1929, just before the stock market crashed and the Great Depression began, I started working for Grover Stokes at the Car Shops. The money was much better—thirty-five cents an hour. I was lettering refrigerator cars, and at that time we were making cars for the Oscar Mayer Packing Company of Mason City, Iowa. Stokes received instructions from Mayer to change the color of the cars from yellow to white.

Stokes had a good supply of yellow paint on hand and told the painters to use up the yellow before they changed to white. When the next shipment of cars was picked up by train (we usually sent them seven or eight at a time), Stokes sent Mayer a telegram: DEAR OSCAR YOUR FLEET OF SNOW WHITE CARS IS ON ITS WAY.

Four or five days later, Stokes received a telegram from Mayer: DEAR GROVER MY FLEET OF SNOW WHITE CARS HAS JUST ARRIVED WITH THE YELLOW JAUNDICE.

I worked there until the Depression closed the plant in 1931.

Showbiz

The English Theater opened in 1922. It was built by the Hammond brothers and was managed by Guy Longest. The film on opening night featured western star Buck Jones in "Ride with Death." There was standing room only and school superintendent S. A. Beals made a short speech.

Initially the theater had only one projector, so the routine was to stop after each reel until the next reel was threaded, the same as at the opera house in years past. Audiences, however, were now more discriminating—or less patient—and the numerous complaints soon forced the brothers to buy a second projector so that the films could be enjoyed without interruption.

Admission was ten cents for kids and twenty cents for adults. On Saturday, which was always a full house, the crowd would be lined up for half a block before the ticket window opened. Patton and Hammond's drugstore also soon bought a popcorn machine and furnished popcorn to the theater. No drinks or candy were sold.

About 1925, Guy decided to install his own popcorn machine at the theater and cut the drugstore out. Understandably, Dr. Guido Hammond failed to see the logic in that and said no. Guy quit. Henry Smith took over as manager and Fred Temple and I got jobs as janitors. We were paid $2.50 a month each, and we could watch the shows for free. Within a year, I worked my way up to running the projectors. My salary zoomed to $15 a month.

We only ran two movies each week, one show each night on Tuesday and Saturday, but there was always something else going on—medicine shows, home talent shows, fiddling contests, political speakers, school graduations, whatever. The theater held about 250 people and was the best place in town for large gatherings.

In 1929, just before the Depression hit, we got talkies. It was the system called Phono-Film. The Hammond brothers had already bought a system called Vita-Phone that synchronized a record with the film, but it didn't work very well. Phono-Film was supposed to be better, since the sound was on the film itself, so the Vita-Phone was taken out before it was ever used. We were one of the first small theaters in southern Indiana to have talking pictures and I can still remember what a thrill it was.

In about 1931, the Hammond brothers' housekeeper had a falling out with Henry Smith and his wife. The result was that Dr. Hammond told me Henry was fired and I was the new manager—at $25 a month. My first assignment was to go to the flour mill where Henry worked during the day, tell him the bad news, and get his keys. Henry and I had been good friends all our lives and I hated to be the one to do that, especially since I knew how much he loved working at the theater. At least he still had a job.

Thomas G. "Hooley" Austin was hired as the new projectionist and I quickly began to appreciate the advantages of being in management. Not only was I making more money—in addition to my day job at the Car Shops—but I could let my new girlfriend, Esther Young, into the theater for free. Henry and I remained friends, but I always felt a little awkward, since we never talked about the theater. Fortunately—for Henry—neither Hammond brother knew anything about the actual running of the theater.

Things went smoothly for several months. Business was good, Esther got to see lots of free movies and shows, and the Depression didn't seem so depressing. One Saturday evening, Hooley and I were getting everything ready for the 7:30 show when we heard the fire siren. I wasn't on the fire department but Hooley was, and since showtime was well over an hour away, I went along to help.

The fire was at a farm west of town and we were among the first to arrive. I helped prevent smoke and water damage by carrying out furniture while the department hosed down the roof. It was over pretty quickly and Hooley and I realized we had better get back to the theater.

Back then fires were more of a social occasion than they are now, and large crowds would turn out not just to help and watch, but to stay afterward and visit. Half the cars in English were now parked on the narrow road between us and the highway back to town—and to the theater, where people were already taking their seats.

Since we had threaded up the projectors before we left, starting the movie was simple. You just turned on the arc lamp, adjusted the carbons, and threw the switch on the projector. Unfortunately, there were only three people in town who knew how to do that and two of us were stuck at the fire. I always wondered what would have happened if Henry would have walked past the theater while Dr. Hammond was pacing back and forth out front, helpless to do anything about his theater full of impatient customers.

By the time Hooley and I threaded our way through the parked cars and reached the highway by driving into ditches and across fields, it was almost 8:00. Dr. Guido was still pacing and the audience was beyond impatient and moving toward unruly when we screeched to a halt in front of the theater. We ran in without a word and got the movie started. I came back down and sheepishly explained about the fire. Dr. Hammond just seemed relieved to be past the crisis.

I think the incident may have helped him realize what an asset Henry had been, especially since he had also booked pictures and taken care of lots of little things I couldn't—or wouldn't—do. Henry was eventually rehired, and everybody was happy, including me, when I gave him back his keys.

And Esther still got to get in for free.

Entertainment

Not all entertainment was at the theater. Traveling medicine shows were always quite an attraction and usually drew big crowds. Of course, it was a free show—as long as you didn't buy anything.

The show I remember most was Dakota Jack's. He came through every summer for years and set up his stage—the back of a flatbed truck—in the street near the Luckett Building. Dakota Jack sold liniment and soap, but his specialty was a tonic made from herbs. He claimed he got the formula for his tonic from an

ENGLISH

One Day Only FRIDAY, Sept. 17

SUN BROTHERS' WORLD'S PROGRESSIVE SHOWS (INC) AND TRAINED WILD ANIMAL TOURNEY

PRESENTING THE HIGHEST PAID AND MOST AMAZING FEATURES OF THE AMUSEMENT REALM

BEST SHOW COMING THIS SEASON

WORLD'S WONDERS AT YOUR DOORS.
105 NEW ACTS.
100 TRAINED ANIMALS.
FINEST PERFORMING ELEPHANTS.
3 BANDS OF MUSIC.
GREATEST AERIALISTS.
WORLD'S CHAMPION GYMNASTS.
25 FAMOUS CLOWNS.
MOST BEAUTIFUL HORSES.
STRANGEST WILD BEASTS.

2 BIG PERFORMANCES DAILY.
AFTERNOON AT 2
NIGHT AT 8
DOORS OPEN AT 1 AND 7 P.M.

AT 12:30 P.M. PRECEEDING THE FIRST PERFORMANCE GREAT NEW FREE EXHIBITIONS ON THE SHOW GROUNDS.

The English News,
September 16, 1915

I vaguely remember seeing this show. It was set up in a field on the Sloan farm. My most vivid memory is of a young boy crossing the tent before the show started. A clown stopped him, took his hat off, and hit him over the head with a fake billy club.

old Indian medicine man in South Dakota and that it could cure almost anything. Make that *absolutely* anything. Like all potent medicines, it was expensive—a dollar a bottle.

Dakota Jack was a big fellow and wore a ten-gallon hat, a buckskin jacket, and a checkered vest with a gold chain. He had a comedian with him who opened the show by singing, dancing, and playing the guitar. Jack was a smooth talker, and by the time he had finished his spiel, people were ready to buy. The comedian walked through the crowd, holding a bottle above his head and yelling, "Who's next?" People would raise their hands and he would cover the whole crowd until all orders were filled. When no more hands went up, he headed back to the stage, yelling, "Let 'em die, Doc! Let 'em die!"

Dakota Jack always stayed about a week and seemed to sell about the same amount of his concoction each night.

Every summer usually saw at least one vaudeville show setting up a tent. One of the first I remember was the Newman and Hamilton Stock Company. Ben Wilkes started coming through in the 1930s, first in a tent at the park and later at the theater. Another popular show was Gracie and Her Gang. They booked the theater for a week, drew an overflow crowd every night, and stayed for another week.

Some entertainment was more spontaneous, but no less popular. About 1925, someone got the bright idea to have a foot race down Main Street between Henry Perkins and Omer "Muck" Brown. This would be a sure crowd-pleaser—each contender weighed in at around three hundred pounds.

Several people chipped in and came up with a prize of five dollars. This was not an insignificant amount. Muck operated a restaurant where bean soup sold for five cents a bowl and Perk got fifteen cents for a haircut. Both men agreed to run. The event was advertised by word of mouth for a couple of days and, by race time, a big crowd was lining both sides of Main Street. The contestants would begin at the railroad tracks, run—or whatever—to the bank at Fifth Street, change direction, and finish back at the railroad.

Just as both men were positioning themselves at the starting line, Muck decided to run barefoot. To the delight of the crowd, he slipped off his shoes and socks and began pawing in the rocks and gravel, explaining that "This will toughen up my feet!" Perk, perhaps having second thoughts about the whole affair, simply suggested, "Let's get this over with." Perk and Muck stepped into position. The crowd grew quiet.

Ready . . . Get set . . . Go!!

Both men moved pretty fast—for their size—and each had his own supporters rooting for him and cheering him on. If the race had been a short dash, it would have been noisy and exciting and over in less than a minute. As it turned out, both men were pretty much spent by the time they got to the bank. Perk started to slow down first, and Muck took that as his cue to ease off. The sprinters quickly became fast walkers. Then not-so-fast walkers. Muck kept his lead and won by about five feet. Perk claimed that Muck had an advantage in that he had run barefoot and demanded that they run again, both wearing shoes. Muck declined. He got the five dollars and a big hand from the crowd.

Talk of the Town

In 1923, the latest, most talked-about technological marvel was the radio. Edgar "Red" Mathers ordered the parts for a radio in kit form, and when he put them together, it worked! This first radio arrived in English just before the Dempsey/Firpo championship fight and I remember a crowd gathering in Red's front yard to hear the broadcast. Red graciously moved his radio onto his front porch, but since the only way to hear was with earphones—and he only had one set—Red listened to the fight and repeated what the announcer said. After a while, he passed the earphones around, but the other listeners didn't relay what was going on. No one seemed to mind, since the big thrill was just getting to hear a voice transmitted through the air.

It wasn't long before Red rigged his radio so it had four sets of earphones, which helped, but the big improvement was the addition of a loudspeaker so everyone could listen at the same time. Red was soon known as "Radio Red."

* * *

Another early radio owner was Ferris Mock. Ferris would have radio parties at night—the only time most stations broadcast—and his parties usually went into the wee hours.

We always enjoyed trying to find different faraway stations, and one night Ferris's brother, Glenn, was dialing and picked up a program we hadn't heard before. The announcer said they were broadcasting from Davis's Pool Room in Leavenworth, Indiana! Everyone was amazed to learn that there was a radio station so close that no one knew about. The announcer went on to say that a showboat had come to town (Leavenworth was on the Ohio River) and the band from the boat was there at the pool room and would play a few musical selections. While the band was playing, Ferris came back into the room and was told about this exciting new discovery. Being the host, Ferris was always coming and going and no one ever noticed that he was never in the room at the same time that the announcer was speaking.

Glenn and I had helped Ferris rig up a microphone and record player in a room down the hall so he could talk and play music through the radio. None of us gave away the joke, and by the next day word had spread about the new radio station in Leavenworth. All the other radio owners in town—about a half dozen—were trying to find the elusive pool hall station.

By the early thirties, Ferris Mock was selling and servicing Philco radios.

Ice

In the twenties, there were no refrigerators—at least not in English—and people used iceboxes. Iceboxes looked more or less like refrigerators, except that instead of the compartment on top *making* ice, it *used* ice, meaning you had to put a chunk of ice in and the lower part would stay cool until the ice melted—usually overnight.

Ice was shipped in by train in a refrigerator car which would be set off on the siding about three or four o'clock in the morning. The druggist, Leo Land, also ran the ice business and four of us would unload the two-hundred-pound blocks about daybreak while it was still cool. It usually took about two hours to unload the ice, haul it to the icehouse, and pack it in sawdust. Land paid us $2.50 each, which was a very good wage. Too bad one load was a six-week supply.

Almost everybody had an icebox and they would come to the icehouse across the alley from Gobbel's barn between six and eight in the morning with their ice hooks and pick up their daily supply for ten cents. Several kids who had wagons made spending money by delivering to their neighbors.

ICE KEEPS MEATS HAPPY

In order to retain its original full flavor, meat must not be deprived of natural moisture. Ice retains moisture. . . there is no drying out. Meats kept in the good old fashioned ice box are juicy, tender and full of flavor. Let us keep your meats happy by delivering ice daily, or as often as your refrigerator needs replenishing.

L. L. LAND

English

Crawford County Democrat, May 26, 1932

Leo Land ran this "come-and-get-it" ice business until about 1927, when John Tucker built another icehouse on the railroad siding. Tucker had a delivery wagon pulled by a big bay horse and he made deliveries all over town.

Not to be outdone, Leo bought a Chevrolet truck and started his own ice delivery. This competition lasted about two years, until Tucker quit the business. Leo continued to deliver, but business slowly fell off as the newfangled mechanical refrigerators replaced the iceboxes.

Bootleg, Moonshine, and White Mule

At midnight on January 28, 1920, The Volstead Act took effect as the Eighteenth Amendment to the Constitution and forbade "the manufacture, sale, or transportation of intoxicating liquors."

I was too young to care about the cutoff date, but it was a popular topic of conversation and I remember Dad and others talking about the saloons closing down. Most everybody tried to stock up while liquor was still for sale, but supplies naturally dwindled. The saloons were also well-stocked for the closing deadline and for a while the pre-Prohibition product from the distilleries was still available—illegally—at inflated prices. Most people knew some way to obtain a bottle or two of commercially produced whiskey. This was called "Bootleg," probably because it had to be concealed—possibly in a boot or trouser leg—rather than carried openly. By 1921, it was commonplace to see passengers stepping off the evening train from Louisville carrying shoe boxes, which conveniently held a pair of contraband bottles.

Obviously, pre-Prohibition liquor would not last forever. The bootleggers, sensing a lucrative market, needed another source of supply.

Enter the moonshiner.

"Moonshine" was homemade illegal whiskey, usually distilled at night—by moonlight—at some hard-to-find location. Setting up a still required very little investment in equipment and moonshining quickly became a tempting pastime, particularly for someone owning a piece of isolated property.

Guido "Doc" Brown once told me when he was first married in the late twenties, he and his wife lived with her father, who was also very poor and barely managed to eke out a living on his old farm. Doc got into moonshining and would be gone most of the night making whiskey and deliveries. Soon he was making plenty of money and would flash his roll of bills in front of his father-in-law. It wasn't long before moonshining was a family business and Doc's father-in-law also had a pocketful of money.

Freshly-distilled whiskey is as clear as water. It is then aged in charred barrels for a year or more, giving it a distinctive reddish-brown color. Locally, the best whiskey came from the German settlements in Dubois County, where they had been making it that way for years. Not willing to go to all that trouble, the moonshiners simply added a couple drops of Coca-Cola syrup to their water-clear product and sold it as Jasper Corn Likker.

In the first year or two of Prohibition, whiskey was selling as high as twenty dollars per quart. (I think pre-Prohibition prices were in the neighborhood of fifty to seventy-five cents per quart, according to the brand and quality.) As more and more moonshiners got into the act, competition got stiffer, prices went down, and quality went up. By the mid-twenties, you could buy pretty good whiskey for three dollars per *gallon.*

During Prohibition, people also made many different kinds of homemade wine. Grape and strawberry were probably most popular. Elderberries were plentiful along the creeks and dandelions grew in most people's yards. Raisinjack was also a favorite. A lot of people bought bottles, bottlecaps, and a capper and made their own beer, called homebrew.

Looking back, I think Prohibition would have been a fine piece of legislation—if it had worked. Prohibition failed because there weren't enough honest men to enforce the law. Not all, but some of the excise agents would lead a raid on a moonshiner, arrest him, destroy his still, and then take his whiskey—minus a small amount for evidence—and turn it over to another bootlegger to sell for half the profits. Some of the local law did the same. For his first offense, a moonshiner usually got ninety days on the penal farm. His second offense was worth six months.

In Case of Prohibition.

If the town goes "dry," buy a gallon of your favorite brand and turn it over to your wife. Do all your drinking at home. Every time you take a drink pay your wife 15 cents. When the first gallon is gone your wife will have $8 to put in the bank and $2 to buy a new supply, each gallon averaging sixty drinks. In ten years at your present rate you will be dead, and your wife will have enough money to go out and marry a decent man.

The English News, August 6, 1915

In about 1928, a restaurant operator in town who was also bootlegging asked me to drive him to Valeen to see his moonshiner, who was several days late on his delivery. When he came back to my car carrying a gallon jug, I was reluctant to take him into town with the moonshine in the car.

"If the sheriff catches us, he could throw us in jail and confiscate my car!"

"Don't worry about the sheriff, I pay him fifteen dollars a week and his eats."

* * *

About the same time, my brother Clyde and I went to visit our grandfather, Ben Roberts, who lived near Smithville. Ben's son, Perry, was a half-brother to Dad and about Clyde's age. Perry asked if we had ever seen a moonshine still operating. We hadn't, so he offered to take us to see the setup of a friend of his. Granddad Roberts already lived about four miles out in the country on a dirt road, and we had to walk along a creek winding up a narrow valley for a mile or so and then off on a spring branch for another quarter-mile. Finally, we saw the smoke from the still.

It was a perfect location in a dead-end gorge—what the oldtimers called a "draw"—where the spring flowed out of a soapstone cliff. Perry's friend and his friend's fourteen-year-old brother were operating the still. Perry suggested we sneak up on them and give them a scare.

Clyde was a part-time deputy sheriff and had his badge with him, so he put it on and stood up where they could see him. They were so busy making moonshine that they didn't notice him until he made some noise to get their attention.

Perry's friend knew he was caught, so he just sat down and waited for the handcuffs. The boy, however, decided to run for it. Having nowhere to go except up the soapstone cliff, he clawed his way halfway up before sliding back down. Desperate, he tried again, with the same result. And again. Finally, he also gave up and sat down with his brother. By this time, we were laughing so hard it was obvious that they were not trapped in a real raid. Perry showed himself, laughing loudest of all.

After we'd been introduced and everyone had calmed down, the fourteen-year-old boy remembered that he had a .32 caliber pistol in his pocket. He had vowed to himself that if the revenuers ever showed up he would not be taken without a fight. When he saw Clyde he forgot all about his pistol and thought only of escaping. Lucky for us.

Their operation was probably pretty typical. They had three or four barrels of mash—a combination of shelled corn, sorghum molasses, baker's yeast, and water—in various stages of fermentation. When the mash smelled right—sort of like beer—it was poured into the copper still, which was a closed container sitting on top of a rock furnace. A fire cooked the mash and the vapor escaped out of a copper tube at the top of the still. The tube was coiled in the running water from the spring, causing the vapor to condense and drip out at the end of the tube. This still was running a stream of moonshine about the size of a wheatstraw. They were catching it in quart fruit jars and pouring it into gallon jugs.

We visited awhile and sampled his commodities. It was warm and pretty rank. As I said, freshly distilled whiskey is crystal clear and looks as harmless as water. It's not. For reasons that become obvious when it's tasted, fresh moonshine used to be known as "white mule." To this day I remember everything about our trip to the still—except the walk back.

Moonshine Raiders

Sometimes when the new boys from the country came to town to start high school, we would pull a prank on them. This was one of the more elaborate ones.

Our victim this time was Charles Austin. My brother Clyde told Charles that he was a special deputy and was going out to make a raid on some moonshiners (this was about 1925) and he needed Charles to accompany him. Charles agreed and Clyde "deputized" him.

Before the raid, Clyde, Ted McMahel, and I went into the woods about a mile north of town and set up a fake moonshine still in a hollow where there was an overhanging cliff with a rock shelf. We stocked it with several lard cans, jugs, bottles, etc. After we piled up wood for a fire, we figured it would look pretty convincing at night. About a hundred feet below the cliff was a ditch with a wash-out about three feet deep—a perfect place to hide. We put some limbs across the ditch and covered it with leaves.

The plan was for Clyde to lead Charles to this spot, where Ted would be hiding in the ditch. Clyde would leave, then Ted would spring up and grab Charles. I would appear with a burlap bag and we would slip the bag over his head, pin his arms to his side, and tie him hand and foot. (This would not be a problem, since we were both bigger than he was.)

Then Clyde would arrive like the cavalry, firing his pistol (loaded with blanks), release Charles, and they would escape in a hail of bullets from *our* pistols (also loaded with blanks). All in all, not a bad evening of entertainment.

About dark, Ted and I went to the location, started the fire, and hid. Soon there was only the moonlight shining through the trees and the glow of the fire. When Clyde arrived with Charles, it all looked very convincing if I do say so myself.

Clyde and Charles crept closer and Clyde positioned his deputy about three feet in front of where Ted was hiding. His instructions were to wait until he heard shots, then come running to help make the arrests. Clyde slipped away into the darkness.

Nothing happened for two or three minutes, then suddenly Ted sprang out and grabbed Charles. I rushed in with the sack and rope. As I said, we were both bigger than Charles was, but there was one thing we hadn't considered: We were fighting for fun; he was fighting for his life. After about ten minutes of kicking, twisting, and rolling around, we were exhausted. When it became obvious that we couldn't handle him, Clyde (who had been nearby watching and enjoying it all) came to the rescue. We turned Charles loose and ran.

As soon as Clyde got Charles to his feet and they headed out of the woods, we came after them, firing our pistols. Every few feet, Clyde would fire back at us. Charles would probably have run all the way back to town if Clyde hadn't stopped him and told him it was a prank. Ted and I caught up with them, winded and laughing so hard we could barely breathe.

We had a lot of fun rehashing the "raid" and we told Charles what a good fighter he was. We all looked at it as a lot of fun and Charles was glad to be "one of the boys."

Homebrew

During Prohibition, coming up with a cold beer and a place to enjoy it was almost always more trouble than it was worth. Almost, but not quite. Some occasions were, however, more troublesome than others.

Late one hot summer afternoon about 1926, Glen Mock and I were hanging out at Hooley Austin's shoe shop and the three of us decided that a cold brew would be just the thing to end the day. Glen and I drove about four miles north of town to a bootlegger we knew named Nolan and bought four fifths of homebrew for a dollar. (Moonshiners seldom produced homebrew, so most bootleggers made their own, just to be able to provide a variety of product. While competition forced the price of moonshine down, homebrew stayed relatively expensive.)

Sometimes bootleggers kept their homebrew cold by storing it in burlap bags submerged in a well or a spring. Occasionally they would keep it in their icebox along with their eggs and milk or at least be willing to chip off some ice shavings to send with their customers. Nolan did none of these, so we arrived back at Hooley's shop a half hour later with four warm bottles of illegal beer. So far so good.

Hooley found a two-gallon stewer in the back of his shop, so he closed up and we drove to the icehouse. We bought a chunk of ice and an icepick, and then headed east to have some privacy, out past the school and finally off on a dirt road to the left. About a mile down the road, we parked in a shady spot, chipped the ice into the stewer, and poured the beer over the ice. Hooley swirled the beer around to get it good and cold before passing it around. It had been over an hour since we had decided to enjoy a cold one and we were all plenty thirsty.

Splat. Suddenly, the stewer was upside-down on the ground, surrounded by a dark stain spreading out in the dirt. I don't remember exactly what Hooley said, but I'm sure it was appropriate and equivalent to what Glen and I were thinking. We drove back to town and stopped for a drink at the sulfur-water fountain that was always flowing next to the stone building. At least it was cold and wet. And cheap. And legal. Just the thing to end the day.

* * *

Sometimes having homebrew within easy reach could also get you into trouble. Early one evening Glen and I were out driving in his Ford Roadster and turned up East Fifth Street so he could stop at his home and change clothes. Glen's father was Henry Mock, a successful and respected attorney who was a one-hundred-percent, no-fooling-around Prohibitionist. We paused in front of Mr. Mock's law office, just off Main Street, but it was closed.

As it happened, we had one bottle of homebrew in the car with us, left over from a recent trip to a bootlegger. "Little Mattie" Moore, a woman who lived upstairs over the law office, was walking past and Glen, in a typical moment of whimsy—and bad judgment—offered the bottle of demon beer to her.

"I don't drink that old homebrew!" she said, offended to her core. Glen suggested something to the effect that it might be an improvement if she did, and drove away. Not far up the street we passed Mr. Mock, headed for his office.

Glen changed clothes in about the same time it took Mr. Mock to reach his office, hear the homebrew story from Mattie, and walk back. He was coming up the sidewalk as we walked out of the house.

"I know you boys have been drinking. I am going to search that car and if I find any whiskey or beer, I will call the sheriff and have you arrested and thrown in jail!" And he meant it. One hundred percent. No fooling around. "Glen, go in the house and bring me a flashlight."

Actually, he didn't even need the flashlight. We had carelessly left the bottle of homebrew sitting on the seat between us. The top of the roadster was down and the bottle was in plain sight. The streetlight was even reflecting off the bottlecap like a small beacon. I could already hear the door of my jail cell slamming shut.

Mr. Mock and I stood there in an icy silence until Glen came back with the flashlight. We all walked toward the car. The bottlecap seemed to be flashing on and off, blinking and beckoning.

Mr. Mock walked right up to the car—and around to the rear, where he told Glen to open the luggage compartment.

In the few seconds while he was digging through the odds and ends in the back, I stepped off the curb, reached across the seat, and picked up the homebrew. Mr. Mock looked up just as I tucked the bottle into my belt behind me. Then he moved to the front of the car, shined the light over the seat, had Glen turn the seat upside-down, double-checked everything . . . and finally gave up.

"You boys are lucky I didn't find anything." And he headed back to his office.

Glen let out a long breath. He hadn't seen me pick up the bottle either. "What in the world happened to the beer?" I turned around and showed him. We got back into the car, drove on up the street, and drank the evidence.

* * *

Since homebrew was so expensive, Glen and I decided to try making it ourselves. We bought a five-gallon jar, some malt, some yeast, some bottles, and we borrowed a capper. All we needed was a secluded place to assemble the ingredients.

Glen lived in the largest house on East Fifth, a street which boasted a number of large homes. After his parents divorced, he and his father and brother moved to the second floor and rented out the first floor. Above the second floor was an attic the size of a hayloft. Since no one ever went up there, it was the perfect secluded spot for a five-gallon brewery—as long as Mr. Mock didn't discover it, call the sheriff, and have us thrown in jail.

We started a batch of water, malt, and yeast working and covered the jar with a cloth to let air in and keep insects out. The attic was unfinished and walled up with poplar boards about two feet wide. We pried off a board and hid our jar in the space between the board and the outside wall.

After about five days, when the brew had quit working, we pulled out the jar and started bottling. It turned out that we had only bought enough bottles for about two-thirds of our batch, so we decided to put the partially-full jar back into the wall and go for more bottles. Somehow we turned the jar over and spilled most of the new beer into the wall space. At least we wouldn't have to buy more bottles.

We had set up our operation right above the kitchen. And, in a few days, a dark stain appeared on the ceiling downstairs. Mr. Mock figured that the roof was leaking—even though it hadn't rained—and hired someone to go up and look around.

We got out of the homebrew business fast.

Spelunkers II

During the Depression, there wasn't much work but lots of free time, so Fred Temple, Paul Mattox, and I put in some time exploring caves. There was a cave near Fargo that I had heard some of the old-timers talking about, so we went to check it out. The entrance turned out to be in a farmer's field, filled with brush to keep the cattle out. The farmer said that no one had been in the cave since he had lived there, but it was okay with him if we went in.

Inside, the cave was high enough to allow us to walk without bending over. There were a lot of initials and dates on the ceiling written in candle smoke. Most of them were from the 1880s and '90s. A spring was flowing through the cave and we decided to follow it and see where it came out. After a while, we began to hear a roaring noise that slowly got louder.

The source of the sound was a small waterfall which poured down into a large pool that blocked our way and stretched as far as we could see. We had to turn back. We had walked quite a way when I began to notice rock formations that didn't look familiar. Springs from other passages flowed into the one we were following and we must have mistakenly followed one of them. Sure enough, there weren't any tracks from when we came in. We were lost.

There was a dirt ridge or backbone on our right that reached almost to the cave ceiling. I crawled up and shined my light into the neighboring passage. There in the sand were our tracks. We squeezed and squirmed over the backbone and down into the next passage. Two and a half hours after we entered, we came back out into the sunlight.

Shot Number Three?

The southwest corner at Fifth and Main was always referred to as "Bill Patton's corner" because his drugstore was there for so many years. At about 9:30 on Sunday evening, July 10, 1928, I was standing at that corner, talking with Hugh Temple and S. A. Beals. The service at the Holiness Church had just ended and Main Street was busier than usual as many of the congregation walked home in the balmy summer air.

I looked up and noticed Cressie Cooper walking toward us. We all knew Cressie well and none of us would have been surprised if he had stopped and chatted awhile. Tonight, however, he seemed not to even notice us as he walked up to the drugstore window and studied the two or three patrons left at the counter. Without so much as a word or nod, Cressie moved on around the corner and crossed the street. Something about him kept my interest as he stopped at the window of Land's Drugstore and looked inside there just as intently. Almost immediately, he went in. My attention returned to Hugh and Mr. Beals. (Yes, I always called him *Mister* Beals.)

We heard a shot, followed immediately by several women screaming. Another shot. More screaming. It sounded like it was coming from Land's. I walked slowly down Fifth on the opposite side of the street to try to see into the drugstore. A third shot. Cressie came out of the drugstore. With a gun in his hand. I stopped.

Cressie walked a few steps west to the alley, stepped into the street, then started running down Fifth and around the corner. The women inside the drugstore were still screaming. Leo Land ran out, yelling for Dr. Gobbel. I stepped into the drugstore and realized who Cressie had been looking for. There on the floor amidst the overturned chairs—and in a pool of his own blood—was Carl Conn. Dead.

I also knew—had known—Carl Conn well. He and Cressie Cooper were friends. Or had been—until Cooper found out that Conn had been seeing his wife. Cooper confronted Conn in the drugstore, drew a pistol in each hand, and shot Conn twice, once in the head and once in the heart, either of which would have been fatal.

But that was only two shots, and I had heard three. Hadn't anyone else heard three? No. All the witnesses swore there were only two shots fired. There were only two wounds in Carl Conn. And everyone knew—as Conn should have—that Cooper was a crack shot. He wouldn't have missed at such close range. No, only two shots. I must have been wrong.

After the shooting, Cooper ran a short distance up Water Street, turned behind the hotel, and hid in the alley near the monument shop. Sheriff Satterfield organized a posse, and when my brother Clyde, who was deputized, returned to the shop to get his gun, Cooper was only a few feet away.

Cooper hid there till about 2:30 in the morning, then made his way to the railroad and started walking, finally catching a freight train as it slowed to make the steep grade west of town. He got off at Taswell and told the night operator, Red Mathers, all about killing Conn. In addition, he warned, there were several more who would taste his wrath before he was caught. And then he headed back toward English.

By the next morning, Cooper's threat was being repeated all over town. That evening, a surprising—and revealing—couple of businesses and homes on Main Street were dark. This had definitely been a crime of passion. And might continue to be.

Early the next evening, Cressie Cooper quietly surrendered himself to Sheriff Satterfield and was taken into custody. The lights came back on. Cooper was eventually convicted of manslaughter and sent to prison.

And, it was learned, as he was backing out of the drugstore after firing the two fatal shots, Cooper put one of the pistols into his belt and it accidentally went off again, into the wall. Shot number three.

Trading Up

I bought my first car when I was eighteen. It was a Ford Model T—or at least it had been at one time. When I got it, the body had been removed and two box seats were bolted to the frame. At least it ran good. I bought it from Volley Smith for twenty-five dollars.

Six months later, I traded with Jim Stallings for a 1925 Chevy coupe. I think I paid thirty dollars difference. This car looked better, but it wasn't much to brag about either.

In 1931 I saw an ad in the paper where Cook Chevrolet had a 1929 Ford Sports Roadster for $165. I figured it was time for a trade, since the battery on my coupe was dead (that meant I had to crank it) and, once it started, it sounded like each rattle and sputter might be its last. Worst of all, I was driving around in second gear a lot because the brakes didn't work. Unfortunately, Cook Chevrolet—and my new roadster—were fifty miles away, in Louisville.

It turned out that most of the trip to Louisville was pretty easy. I could use third gear on the highway as usual and, since the towns along the way were no bigger than English and had little traffic, I could shift into second when necessary and safely coast through the intersections. The only problem was that changing gears required several violent attempts to move the shift lever, with grindingly louder complaints from the car, and increasingly rude comments from myself. It was exhausting and, with the inevitable amused smiles from passersby, embarrassing.

After I got into Louisville, I stayed in second gear since there was suddenly lots of traffic—and lots of traffic lights. I was doing a pretty good job of speeding up and slowing down so I could catch the green, but I knew if I hit a light on red, the chances were good that I'd probably hit something else as well.

About three blocks from Cook's, the light changed just as I got there and I rolled helplessly into the intersection. Cars stopped, horns blew, and passersby smiled their amused smiles. Second gear had never seemed so slow. Cook's had never seemed so far away. As soon as I found enough stopping room at a curb, I pulled over and parked.

I walked the rest of the way and finally got to see my roadster. No car ever looked so good. I told the salesman about my Chevy and he volunteered to drive it to the lot for me. He said he didn't mind driving a car with no brakes. We walked back and he got behind the wheel. I felt a lot better, knowing he was used to driving in the city, and I figured I'd learn something by watching what he did.

We took off and caught the first light on green. He even used third gear. When the second light turned red as we approached, I realized that his strategy was to shift to second so we would slow down. He tried. BRRPPP! Again. GGGRRKKKK! Fortunately, there was no cross-traffic and we made it through the intersection alive. He pulled into the lot and we coasted to a stop. The salesman took a deep breath and said he would never try that again.

He allowed me twenty-five dollars for the coupe and gave me what was an old sales pitch even then: The roadster had been owned by an elderly man and his wife and they only drove it to church and back on Sunday. Considering what we had been through together, I thought he might have spared me that, but it could have been true since the rumble seat looked brand-new and the car ran great.

I drove back to English in style.

I had been working at the Car Shops, making about fifteen dollars a week, but the Depression was making it tough for them to keep operating and they started getting behind with our pay. Every payday was a few dollars short with a promise it would be made up next time. Next time it was the same story. They finally closed owing me sixty dollars. My car payments fell behind and I lost my roadster. That was a blow.

A year or so later, my brother Codger sold me another Chevy coupe for seventy-five dollars. This was a later model and it ran much better. I was back on wheels and have never been without a car since.

The Fire Department

In about 1928, Paul Mattox and I were pouring concrete for a sidewalk at the Hammond brothers' home on North Main. I noticed that a fire had just started burning around the chimney of a two-story dwelling over on Court Street. Harold "Hokie" Conn, who owned the dwelling, ran a poultry house nearby, so I told Paul to round up some help and I ran to warn Hokie.

When I ran into the poultry house, "Pert" Enlow, the boy who worked there, was sitting in the office with his feet up on the desk, reading. I asked where Hokie was.

"He's not here."

"His house is on fire!"

"Yeah."

And he just kept on reading. I ran back through the poultry house and to the kitchen door of the house that was on fire. Hokie's mother was washing dishes. I told her not to get excited, but the roof of her house was on fire. She didn't get excited—she just stared at me the way Pert had done. I assured her that help was on the way. She still didn't say a word.

I ran outside, found an extension ladder, and got it set up. Within minutes, Paul returned with Leo Land and a couple of others, and we got the fire put out without much damage.

Just when it was about all over, I turned around and there was Pert, watching. "Gee," he said, "I thought you were only kidding!"

* * *

At that time the fire department consisted of a pushcart and about a hundred and fifty feet of hose, operated by whoever was available. That was good enough for small fires, but hardly adequate for serious emergencies.

The serious emergency didn't happen until the spring of 1932.

Fire broke out in Jim Turley's Hardware Store about 10:00 P.M. The building was three stories with a full basement and was sided with roofing paper. It made for a really hot fire and it was quickly obvious that the fire department's pushcart was useless. The entire business district was in danger. The French Lick and Paoli fire departments were called, but by the time they arrived the hardware store and four dwellings were destroyed. Fortunately, three or four more buildings that had caught on fire were saved and the fire didn't spread into the main business district.

The Town Board decided that English needed more fire protection. They purchased a 1932 model Seagrave fire truck for about $13,000 and a volunteer fire department was organized.

Less than a year later, about two o'clock on a cold morning in March, 1933, the fire department got a call for help from Leavenworth. Fire had broken out in the C. G. Austin Grocery on Nelson Street. It also happened that the Ohio River was the highest it had been in twenty years and much of the town was flooded.

My brother Codger and I were awakened by the fire siren and decided to make the run with the fire department. We were driving a 1928 model Chevy coupe and pulled into Leavenworth just minutes ahead of the firemen.

A crowd had gathered at the upper end of Nelson Street, which was mostly covered with water. Because we arrived first, they thought I was the fire chief and asked where I wanted the fire truck. I pointed to a couple of cars that should be moved so the truck could back down to the edge of the water to drop in the suction line for pumping. When the truck showed up with its siren blaring, the street was clear and they soon got set up and went to work.

The grocery was pretty well burned to the waterline by the time the fire department arrived, but other nearby buildings that had caught fire were saved. Somebody from a restaurant that was not in the high water brought me a big container of hot coffee—since I was in charge—and as the boys came in wet and cold I would pour them a cup. Bill Alexander, who lived up the street, also handed me a gallon jug of wine. I started filling the cups with wine, which seemed to give the boys an extra lift.

I never did tell them I wasn't the fire chief.

Wheat Harvest in Kansas

In July 1930, the Great Depression was on. It was almost impossible to find a job, and money was hard to come by. Glen and Ferris Mock, Fred Mathers, and I decided to drive to Kansas, where a job during wheat harvest paid a whopping four dollars per day, plus room and board.

The morning we left I had fifty dollars—fifteen of my own and thirty-five I borrowed from Leo Land, the druggist. By dark we were in southern Illinois, where we pulled off the road for the night.

Fred had rigged his 1926 Star touring car with a bed made out of boards that fit between the windshield and the top of the back seat. It folded up into three sections that were hinged together and we carried it on the right front fender, where it was wired to the car. It was only about five feet wide and you can imagine four men trying to sleep in such close quarters. When one of us tried to turn over, we all had to move at the same time. Besides that, it was rock hard. After a couple of hours trying to sleep, Glen and I got out and slept on the ground. It felt much better.

The next morning we got up and fixed breakfast from food we had brought with us, got the bed wired back on the fender, and headed for St. Louis. We figured if we could get through the big city by noon, we could make it into Kansas that day. The roads were not too good—mostly gravel—but we averaged about thirty miles per hour, which was fast enough. We arrived in St. Louis pretty well on schedule.

We were driving through the main part of the city on a brick street which was pretty bumpy. All at once the folding bed fell off into the street. Fred started to stop, but we all said to keep going. We agreed we didn't need the bed, so Fred drove on and left our sleeping facilities in St. Louie.

About four o'clock that afternoon, we crossed into Kansas. The roads were a little better and we were driving a little faster, maybe around forty. Suddenly we hit a jump-off in the road and broke a spring leaf (the forerunner of shock absorbers). There was a small town about a mile on down the road where we limped into a garage. We were delayed about three hours while we got the spring replaced. Fred wanted us to pay part of the bill, but we reminded him that our agreement was that we paid for the gas and oil and he furnished the car. He had to pay—three dollars and fifty cents.

About dark, we stopped at a place where they had cabins for rent. Glen and I rented a cabin for a dollar fifty. Sheets and pillow cases were extra, so we did without. At least we had a mattress and pillows. Fred and Ferris slept in the car.

The next afternoon we arrived in Macksville, Kansas. We figured we would have to split up to find work, but we made a pact: When we finished with the wheat harvest, we would get together and head for California. (This was not the plan when we left English, it was something we came up with on the way out.)

There was a man named George Cummins who had moved to Macksville from English in 1925 and we looked him up when we got to town. Ferris and Glen stayed with him and his family till they found jobs, but I didn't want to feel like a freeloader, so I found other accommodations—Fred and I slept in the car at a small park on the edge of town.

During the day our routine was to sit around on a curb in downtown Macksville with other laborers and wait to be hired by the farmers who came by. After about three days of this, Glen and I were hired by a farmer named Miller who lived near St. John, about ten miles away. It was about a week before the wheat would be ripe enough to harvest, so he put us to work doing odd jobs, listing corn, fixing fences, cutting the heads off the rye he had in the field for his seed wheat, and the like. Ferris found a job on a farm about two miles from where we were, and Fred was working about fifteen miles away.

One day when Farmer Miller and his family had gone into

town and left us working in the fields, a big storm came rolling in—black clouds, lightning, thunder, strong winds. We headed for the house, but remembering that Kansas was known for tornadoes, we started looking for a safer place. The closest farm with a storm cellar was about a quarter of a mile west. We decided to try and make it over there, but the storm was coming from the west and we couldn't buck the wind.

There was an open fruit cellar near the house where a building had blown away several years earlier, so we made a dash for it. It had about a foot and a half of water in it, but we waded in and got down next to the west wall until the storm blew past. When we crawled out of that cellar, we looked like a couple of drowned rats.

Miller and his family were on their way back when the storm hit and they had stopped at a neighbor who had a storm cellar. He said he watched the storm pass right over his house and he thought the wind was going to take it, but it didn't dip down as it passed by. If it had, we would probably have gone along for the ride.

When we finally started combining wheat, Glen drove the tractor that pulled the combine and I drove a Model T Ford truck hauling wheat. We combined the ten acres of seed wheat first, which was his best yield, making about fifty bushels per acre.

I trucked the wheat to a metal bin and then scooped it out. That was the hardest and hottest part of the job. Then I would rush back to the field where the combine would be waiting with another load. It took us about a day to finish with the seed wheat, then I started hauling the wheat to an elevator in town. During the Depression, farmers were only getting 35 to 36 cents a bushel for wheat that normally would have brought between two and three dollars. When I brought the first check back and handed it to Farmer Miller, he just looked at it and shook his head.

After about ten days, Glen began to get homesick. I talked him out of leaving a couple of times, but one morning he got up and packed his bag. I tried to get him to stay until we finished (only another week), but his mind was made up. He rode into town with me when I took a load of wheat and caught a bus for English.

Ferris finished working two days after Glen left, then came over and helped us at the Miller farm.

Finally, the last day of wheat harvest was over. We got a good night's sleep, ate a big breakfast, and headed for town with money in our pockets, anxious to find Fred and start for California. (I was especially excited, since I had decided I would not just go west to visit, but I would probably stay and seek my fortune.)

When we got to town, we asked George Cummins if he had seen Fred. Yes, he had, at a garage in town almost a week earlier, buying a five-gallon can of oil and saying he was headed for California. Alone. Without us. Needless to say, I was pretty disappointed. We briefly considered heading west on our own, but decided to look for a way back to English.

George knew of a man named Mathers and his sister who were from Terre Haute and were in town visiting relatives. We looked them up and found out they were leaving the next day, but going back by way of southern Missouri, through the Ozarks. They said we were welcome to come along if we would pay for the gasoline and oil. That was okay with us. So much for California!

Four days later, we arrived at Mt. Carmel, Illinois, caught a train to English, and arrived home at about four in the morning. My bed had never felt so good. The next day, my dad, who had been to Macksville ten years earlier, wanted to hear all about my adventure. I didn't tell him I had almost become a Californian.

Fred pulled back into town about six weeks later. He had made it to California with about $1.85 left. He picked pears to get enough money to come home. On his way back across the desert, he got caught in a sandstorm and crawled under his car while the top blew off and disappeared into the desert. He almost had to sell his car to make it back. When he arrived in English, he was broke, almost as beat-up as his car, and well-sunburned.

When we asked him why he took off without us, he said he didn't know. He guessed he was just in a big hurry to get started.

He was sorry and he wished now that he would have waited, but he just couldn't explain why he did it. (This would be a continuing joke between us for the next fifty-odd years. Until his death a couple of years ago, he would see me and ask if I still wanted to go to California.)

If Fred hadn't left us in Kansas, I might have gone to California and stayed—or I might not have. We'll never know. As it turned out, I was gone about a month, had a memorable adventure, and ended up thirty dollars ahead. All in all, one of my better memories of the Great Depression.

Buried Treasure

Around 1931, my grandfather, Ben Roberts, was visiting us and told a story about an old-timer he had known back in the 1880s who had made a lot of money dealing in hogs and cattle. Most of his transactions were in gold, and, when he died, his money was never found.

Granddad told us about a dream he had had years before. He had dreamed the same dream three nights in a row and in the dream he saw where the old-timer's gold was buried. He believed in those dreams and was convinced he could find the location. Dad, my brother Codger, and I agreed to take him.

We all got into the car and Granddad directed us to a spot on the Jericho Road, where we parked. We walked down a long hill into a valley until we crossed what was left of the old Brownstown Road. It hadn't been used since the 1890s, but you could still see traces of the ruts cut down by wagon wheels. We followed the old road for a short distance until we came to a small cliff. There were boulders and some other signs that Granddad recognized. This was the location from his dreams.

My dad had brought a gold bracelet of my mother's to use as a divining rod. He cut a small limb, fastened the bracelet to one end, and then held the other end as he walked back and forth. The gold bracelet bobbed up and down several times before he decided on the most likely spot to dig.

We hadn't brought any digging tools, so we marked the spot and went home. No one dreamed about gold that night.

It was July and hot, and when we returned the next day Dad and Granddad stayed in the car while Codger and I went for the gold. It was high noon when we reached the marker, which was not even close to any shade. The ground was hard and rocky, and after about an hour of digging, we were filthy and exhausted and only down about three feet with no gold or any signs of gold. We decided to rest awhile, and then we decided to give up. We trudged back up the hill.

Granddad was expecting us to show up with a pot of gold, and he was sadly disappointed. He was convinced we hadn't dug deep enough. I didn't tell him, but I had never put much stock in the story in the first place. As far as I was concerned, the best part was that he had even found the Brownstown Road and the spot he had dreamed about.

But, if he was right and we just hadn't dug deep enough . . .

Another Ghost Story

In the early 1930s, I worked for my father in his monument business. When someone died, the surviving spouse usually bought a monument with both inscriptions. When the survivor passed away, I would go to the cemetery, locate the monument, and cut the death date with a hammer and chisel.

Usually I waited until I had two or three dates to cut in the same area so I could cut them all in one trip. On this particular run, I had three dates to cut in the Alton area. I had finished two and the third was in an old cemetery out by itself and mostly surrounded by woods. By the time I got there, it was late in the afternoon.

I finally located the monument, knelt down, and started to work, hoping I could get done before it got dark, because the old cemetery was spooky even in daylight. It typically took about two hours to finish a death date, and by the time I was gathering up my tools to leave, there was just barely enough light to allow me to find my way out.

Just then I heard some popping and cracking. I turned to listen and realized that the sound was coming from the grave behind me. Looking closer, I could see the ground over the grave starting to crack open. I've never believed in ghosts, but I have to admit my heart was definitely beating faster.

It was only a mole working. There were flowers growing on the grave and the mole was making the roots pop and crack.

I gathered my tools and was glad to get back to my car.

A Saturday Night Kind of Town

In the 1930s, English was the place to be on Saturday night.

By 6:00 P.M., you couldn't find a parking place anywhere on Main Street. The sidewalks were bustling and all the business places were full. The Holiness Church was usually starting a half-hour street service about then, appropriately located near the Green Lantern Tavern. They always drew a crowd, but the beer drinkers would manage to elbow their way through. The jukebox in the beer-joint would sometimes almost drown out the singing and preaching, but the worshipers didn't seem to mind.

About 7:00, the butcher shop and hardware stores would close and by 8:00, the clothing stores and barber shops were shutting down.

By 9:00, the theater crowd was out and they either went home or stopped in at one of the taverns. The grocery stores were open to accommodate last-minute shoppers till about 9:00, then they locked up for the night. Except for Charley Turley. After 9:00, Turley's stopped being a grocery store and became a card parlor. Charley was a serious Rook player, and if he was involved in a game, you could forget about being waited on. He did, however, keep a big round block of longhorn cheese and, for a dime, you could have all you wanted, crackers and mustard included.

By 10:00, the restaurants and drugstores were closed and most of the activity was in the saloons or at Turley's. By 1:00, most of these hangers-on were calling it a night, but that didn't mean Main Street was quiet. There were several benches along the street and a few night owls were usually hanging out there until the wee hours.

Sometimes a few who were the most primed would start to sing. The people who lived in upstairs apartments nearby would have their windows open in the summer, and before long someone would lean out and yell, "Shut up and go home so we can get some sleep!" To which one of the singers might reply, "We're just trying to sing you folks to sleep!"

Short Story

About 1933, a farmer named Benton Standiford decided to try a new line of work, so he bought Claude Brown's restaurant on Main Street. Shortly after he opened, three well-dressed women tourists who were passing through town stopped and asked if they could use his rest room.

If they had asked to use his toilet, or even inquired about his inside plumbing, Benton would have known what they wanted. As it was, he thought "rest room" was just some big-city phrase for a place to relax when you were tired.

Benton told the ladies to "Just sit down around here anywhere."

The Disaster That Might Have Been

One cold winter afternoon about 1933, Knofel Scott, Gerald Smith, Harry "Tub" Temple, and I were loafing around the big cast-iron stove in the back part of Leo Land's drugstore. Leo suddenly decided that the fire in the stove wasn't burning to suit him.

"I'll make it burn!" he said, and picked up a glass gallon jar about three-quarters full of white gasoline that he used in a gas lantern. We thought he was kidding, since everyone knows how dangerous white gasoline can be. But when he unscrewed the cap and started toward the stove, we decided not to take any chances. We got out of the way. Gerald and I moved toward the front of the store, Scotty and Tub headed for the back door.

Leo wasn't kidding. When he opened the door and dashed some of the gasoline into the stove, the fire licked out and caught the jar on fire in his hands. If he dropped it, the whole back room would be engulfed in wall-to-wall flames. (Remember that the post office was on one side, a clothing store was on the other, and the back room was full of wallpaper and paint. This was probably the worst place in town to drop a gallon-sized Molotov cocktail!)

Leo started for the back door, fumbling with the burning jug and stringing a path of gasoline and fire behind him. His flaming trail first ignited a rack full of wallpaper, and then the labels on several cans of paint. Fortunately, Tub was already at the back door and had it open by the time Leo got there. Leo immediately threw the jug away—and up against the coal house out back, setting that building on fire.

There was now a wall of fire from the stove to the back door and all the way to the ceiling. Scotty grabbed a minnow bucket full of water that was sitting in the sink near him and dashed it along the floor, putting out most of the fire. Gerald and I managed to knock the fire off the wallpaper and paint labels and stamp it out. Then we all grabbed buckets and carried water to the fire out back. Soon, it was all over, except for the soot, the smoke, and the mess. Surprisingly, Leo's hands weren't badly injured and we all had a chance to catch our breaths.

I told Leo that when Scotty threw the water, I was about to take down the overcoat that was hanging nearby and try to smother the fire. "That was my new overcoat!" he said. "It's a good thing you didn't. I'd have killed you!"

Backfire

About a year after the white gas incident, my brother Clyde traded for a German Luger. It was different from an ordinary handgun and very few people in English had ever seen one. I thought of a way we could have some fun with it.

I dug out a repeating cap pistol I had had for years. For a cap gun, it was extra loud, and sounded as convincing as a real pistol. That evening, Clyde and I took our guns down to Leo Land's drugstore.

Only Leo and Tub Temple were there. Clyde had the Luger tucked conspicuously in his belt and I had the cap pistol in my pocket. Clyde told about trading for it that day and said he couldn't even figure out how to tell if it was loaded or not. Maybe Tub could help him.

Just as Clyde handed over the Luger, I slipped the cap gun out of my pocket and fired it. Leo and Tub both jumped and dodged and had a good scare. I showed them the cap gun and we all thought it was pretty funny. Tub, having been the butt of the joke, took the Luger and waited for the next victim.

Before long, a cigarette salesman by the name of Fink stopped in. He sat down in Leo's chair, put his feet up on the desk, and started to read the paper. Tub wandered over, staggering as if he were drunk. He used Clyde's story about trading for the Luger and not knowing if it was loaded. He waved it around in front of Fink, who kept warning Tub to be careful. I figured Fink would eventually try to take the Luger away from Tub, and when he finally reached for it, I fired the cap pistol. Fink jolted back in the chair, tried to get up, fell back again, struggled to his feet, and actually stood there checking to see if he'd been shot—in spite of the fact that we were all laughing uproariously. He didn't appreciate the joke and left muttering to himself.

Leo started to say something about maybe this wasn't such a funny idea after all just as Ferris Mock came into the drugstore. We all knew Ferris was a good sport, so Tub went into his drunken gunman routine again.

This time, we all got into the act by yelling at Tub to be careful and to stop waving a loaded gun around. When Ferris walked into the middle of all this, it must have seemed pretty convincing—he immediately headed for the back door. Not wanting Ferris to miss out on any of the fun, I fired the cap pistol. Clyde yelped as if he had been shot.

Ferris panicked. He tried to get out the back door, but it was locked. While he was frantically tugging and pulling, I fired another cap. More yelling. Tub staggered toward Ferris with the gun outstretched. Ferris turned around . . .

And everybody froze. One look at Ferris's face told us we had gone too far. Tub sobered up real fast and lowered the Luger. I showed Ferris the cap gun and we explained that it was all a joke. We sat him down in a chair, but he was still shaking. Leo brought him a drink. Slowly, Ferris calmed down and the color returned to his face. We waited in silence to see what he'd say when he could finally speak.

Eventually, Ferris just stood up and walked out the front door without saying anything. He never mentioned the incident again. And neither did we.

The Bear

In the spring of 1934, a circus came to English. One of its attractions was a full-grown black bear named Ruby. Ruby's cage was so small she couldn't even stand up or turn around. My brother Clyde felt sorry for her and bought her for thirty-five dollars.

We built a pen under a shade tree near the monument shop. It was about ten feet square, with willow poles six inches apart on three sides and a front made out of inch-and-a-half pipe. The concrete floor was concave to hold water for a wallow. When we let Ruby into the pen, she immediately took a bath and we could tell she enjoyed the freedom of her new home. Even though she was pretty tame (Clyde would pet her, although I never did), we put a fence about three feet out from the pen so kids wouldn't get too close.

The grocery stores saved leftover produce for her and people brought in sorghum that had turned to sugar—her favorite. The building next door was a restaurant, and Zena Hicks Turner, the lady who ran it, lived in the rear. Her bedroom was only about thirty feet from Ruby's den.

One night there was a terrific storm—thunder, lightning and a hard wind. About two o'clock in the morning, Zena was awakened by the sound of a window breaking. She was sure the bear had escaped and she could just see it crawling through the window to get her. She waited with the covers pulled over her head until the storm finally subsided—and the bear failed to appear—before she discovered that a limb had blown off a tree and through her window.

That fall a carnival came to town and wanted to buy Ruby. Not being very sure of how to provide for her during her winter hibernation (and seeing a chance to have some fun), Clyde agreed to sell—with one provision: They had to take her out of the pen and lead her to the park at two o'clock the next afternoon. That would be no problem, they said. After all, they were professional animal handlers.

The news of Ruby's departure traveled fast and by the next afternoon there must have been three hundred people waiting on Main Street. I had a ringside seat from up on the monument platform next to the pen. The handlers from the carnival showed up right on time with a collar that had a chain fastened to each side. The plan was to cut two of the pole bars out and put the collar on her when she poked her head through.

But apparently Ruby was not very happy at the thought of being evicted, and came charging out through the hole instead, causing the "professional animal handlers" to drop the collar and run—along with three hundred frightened onlookers. One fellow told me later that, as he turned to run, he fell and another man fell on top of him. He thought sure the bear had him.

Ruby was now between the pen and the outside fence. Clyde grabbed one of the poles and forced her back against the pen, holding her there until the handlers realized they weren't being chased. They returned—along with three hundred cautious onlookers.

Ruby still wasn't about to go peacefully. With one handler on each side pulling the chain taut, she fought all the way to the park. The crowd followed, but stayed well back just in case she got loose again.

The carnival left town that night and I kind of missed Ruby and felt sorry for her, but at least the cage she had when she left town was bigger and more comfortable than the one she had when she arrived.

The Penny Detective

Late in 1935, the local commissioned agent for the Socony Vacuum Oil Company (later Mobil Oil) was fired when he came up about $2000 short. My brothers and I talked about one of us taking the job. Clyde had taken over our dad's monument shop, Codger was working for the state, and I was once again projectionist at the movie theater. After several meetings with the district supervisor and his field man, we decided that I would be the new gasoline distributor. I traded my '28 Nash sedan in on a new ton-and-a-half Chevy truck. In March of 1936, I drove to Indianapolis and had a 600-gallon tank installed. I was in the oil business.

I started with about a dozen local farm customers and only two service stations where I delivered gas and oil, one on South Main Street in English and one in Marengo. There was a bulk plant in Salem, and I had to make the eighty-mile round trip almost every day to load my tank truck. Sometimes it was more than just inconvenient. I carried motor oil in five-gallon cans, which I filled by hand from fifty-gallon barrels. The barrels were on a platform about three feet high and I would set my cans on the ground and then tilt one of the heavy barrels over on its side to fill them. It was a clumsy operation at best, and one day when I was in a hurry, I accidentally opened the faucet on the barrel as I tilted it. At least a half gallon went down my open shirt collar and I was oiled to my shoes. I had to drive all the way home slipping and sliding in my oily clothes.

The station at English also included a small market and should have been profitable, but the owner got into debt, couldn't pay his bills and, as a result, Codger and I ended up taking over the business. We hired Roy Temple to run it.

Included in the equipment that came with the station were two slot machines of the one-armed-bandit variety in the back room. One was a nickel machine and the other took pennies.

One evening shortly after we had taken over the station, the lady who lived across the street, Clara Lewis, thought she heard the sound of glass breaking. Roy had closed the station, so she watched and waited and soon saw a green Dodge coupe drive away from the back. Clara walked uptown, looking for Roy, Codger, or me. She found Esther and me having dinner at a restaurant. I took Esther home, went to the station, and immediately called Codger.

Someone had broken through the back window and stolen the one-armed bandits.

By the time Codger arrived, I had determined that the only other things missing were some cigarettes and candy, along with a cigar box half full of pennies that we kept to make change for the penny bandit. When we got flashlights and went looking around out back, we found both one-armed bandits in the weeds, damaged, but not broken into. We brought them back in, covered the window, and decided not to call the sheriff, seeing as how we were out less than ten dollars—and our slot machines were, after all, illegal. We went home and that was that.

Except . . . I remembered that sometimes when the penny slot machine jammed, we poked the coins in with an ice pick.

Quite a few of the stolen pennies had distinctive scratches on them. The next morning I went to the bank and asked Louie Helmbrecht, the cashier, to watch for anyone bringing in pennies like that. A couple of days later he called me. The pennies had showed up, brought in by . . . the theater.

Ada Longest sold tickets at the theater and I asked her if anyone had recently paid for admission with pennies. Yes, the night before, a young man had paid for himself and his date with forty pennies. She told me his name and I knew I had found our thief. He was the kid brother of one of my customers. He worked in Indianapolis, but when he was in town to see his girlfriend, he occasionally bought gasoline at our station, for his green Dodge coupe.

I told Codger and we agreed not to say anything about it, although I wondered what I would do the next time the one-armed-bandit bandit stopped in for gas. I never found out. He still visited English, but he never came back to our station.

Spelunkers III

In about 1936, my brother Codger was employed by the State Highway Engineering Department. He was working with a contractor building State Road 62. About three miles east of Leavenworth, while making a cut through a hill, the equipment dug into a cave. When he came in from work that evening, he told me and Roy Temple about the discovery and explained that it was in the middle of the right-of-way and would be sealed in two or three days. We got our lights and drove down to look it over.

It was pretty steep getting down, but well worth the effort. The cave was limestone and beautiful, with formations of all kinds, from the size of a pencil to four or five feet through. In one place there was a line of stalagmites and stalactites that looked like prison bars. They reached from floor to ceiling and the ceiling was fifteen or twenty feet high. (One way to remember which is which is that stalac*tites* are stuck *tight* to the ceiling and stalag*mites might* make it.)

That evening we were in the cave for only about three hours. There were formations of all shapes and sizes and passages that led off in other directions. We were frustrated because it would have been a wonderful cave to explore and we knew we would only be able to see a small part of it. It was quite a thrill to walk through a beautiful cave that no human eye had ever seen before.

The next evening my brother said the cave would be capped and sealed the following day. This time we returned with hammers and chisels and managed to carry out several pieces of formations. (Normally, I wouldn't take formations from a cave, but under the circumstances, it seemed okay.) We brought back fourteen or fifteen pieces and kept them on display in our service station for about six months. Eventually we gave them to one of the owners of Wyandotte Cave and he put them on display. As far as I know, they are still there.

The Crow

Sometime in the late 1930s, Mary Reasor caught a young crow and Mrs. Mayo Newton split its tongue so it could talk. Mary named the crow Pete. Pete had a limited vocabulary, but the words came out loud and clear. The phrase he used most was "Where ya goin'?" Pete became something of a local celebrity and whenever he showed up, everyone would stop and listen.

Pete had a daily routine. He would follow the kids to school each morning and escort them home in the afternoon. "Escort" meant that he would swoop down and nip at their heads, fly ahead and wait till they had passed, then repeat the maneuver. After seeing the kids safely to school, Pete always came home by a certain route and made several stops.

One of the stops on his route was at Dr. Gobbel's office, where cracked walnuts would be waiting for him on the porch. One morning Dr. Gobbel walked out on the porch to say goodbye to a lady patient and, as she went down the steps to the street, she heard someone plainly say, "Where ya goin'?" She stopped, looked both ways, and saw no one. When she got to the street, she heard the same strange voice again: "Where ya goin'?" Since it was obvious to her that the culprit could only be Dr. Gobbel, she gave him a look that plainly required an explanation if he was ever to see her again as a patient. The doctor smiled and pointed to the roof. The woman looked and, as if on cue, old Pete swelled up and voiced his favorite phrase again.

As time passed, Pete learned some new tricks—and became quite a nuisance. For instance, he began to collect things and take them home. One of his favorites was clothespins. When he pulled them off clotheslines, the wash would fall on the ground.

Or . . .

In those days, milk was delivered in glass bottles with a paper cap pressed into the neck. Pete liked to punch a hole in the cap with his beak and drink the cream that settled on top.

And . . .

The young boy who delivered newspapers couldn't tell the difference between being "escorted" and being "attacked." Sometimes he would fall down on his back and scream while fighting Pete off with a paper.

Pete's admirers began to dwindle.

One morning Pete abandoned his usual routine and hung around the school. He sat in the windows, looked into the classrooms, talked, and generally disrupted the classes.

Pete had finally stepped over the line. In a careless moment he got caught by the janitor, who performed the ultimate indignity:

he clipped Pete's wings. Then to make matters even worse, the janitor let him go. For the first time in his life, Pete had to walk home.

Home was only about a mile away—as the crow flies—but on foot it turned out to be a lot longer. After three days of crossing streets, running down alleys, dodging cats and dogs, and maybe even getting lost, Pete finally made it home, rumpled, ruffled, and much the worse for wear. Mary put him in a cage and that was the end of his troublemaking.

The Monkey

The oil business was not the best-paying job I had ever had, but with the country in the depths of the Depression I was at least employed and pretty much my own boss. In June of 1937, I had a reliable car, $200 in the bank, a dependable income, and a steady girlfriend. The next logical step was . . .

On the 19th, Esther and I stood nervously in front of Leonard Cummins, an elder and part-time minister at the Christian Church. We had decided not to tell anyone—it was pretty much spur-of-the-moment—and so we were married in Reverend Cummins's home.

During the Depression, many of the couples being married could just barely afford the license fee, let alone the cost of wedding bands. Unless told otherwise, ministers usually ignored the part of the ceremony about exchanging rings so as not to embarrass them. I had bought Esther a ring, but I forgot to tell Reverend Cummins. He never mentioned it, and we were outside and on our way back to the car before I remembered and slipped it on her finger.

It was Saturday night of the Reunion, so we went to the

dance at the park and told everyone the news. We stayed with Clyde that night and told Dad the next morning.

* * *

A few months later, Esther and I were visiting relatives in Princeton. My brother-in-law and I went for a walk and met a fellow leading a monkey on a chain. He said he was willing to sell the monkey for twelve dollars, so I bought it. The monkey's name was Jocko.

When it came time to return to English, I put Jocko in the back seat, but he seemed to prefer being in the front with us. Esther preferred that he not be in the car at all. One of them would have to ride in the trunk. Jocko lost.

Esther had a small dog at home named Poogie, who turned out to not be particularly fond of Jocko either. And likewise. It was quickly obvious that Jocko would not be a house pet.

I put up a pole about six feet high behind the station, built a box on top, and fixed a chain long enough so Jocko could play on the ground. I figured if a dog came along and bothered him, he could climb the pole and get away.

An escape route for Jocko wasn't necessary. While he was docile and lovable with me, he got a little crazy around other animals. Dogs and cats careless enough to trespass near his domain were confronted with a snapping, snarling, spitting monster. Jocko soon had the back of the station all to himself.

Except for a neighbor boy named George Sloan. George, who was about fourteen and the great-grandson of James Sloan, started coming by almost every day just to tease Jocko. Unlike the dogs and cats, George figured out that if he stayed just beyond the reach of Jocko's chain, he would be safe. He would make grunting noises and strange faces and kick dirt and Jocko would get really mad and lunge at him, always being pulled up short by the chain. I was afraid this might injure Jocko or make him mean even to me and I would tell George not to do it. He would leave, but a day or so later I would hear a commotion out back and George would be at it again.

One day I heard George teasing Jocko, but I didn't say anything. When he finally got tired—and Jocko was seething mad—George walked around to the front of the station, sat down on one of the benches, and started chatting with a couple of fellows who were already there. I unhooked Jocko's chain and led him around to join them.

Jocko immediately jumped into George's lap, grabbed him by his suspenders, and started hissing and snapping right in his face. Jocko was trying to bite him, but George was leaning back as far as he could and I was holding the chain so he was just out of reach. George started begging me to please take the monkey off. He would never tease him again. Please, please, please. I told him I would take the monkey off this time, but if there was a next time, I wouldn't. He swore he would never do it again. Never. Please, please.

I had a hard time getting Jocko to turn loose, but when he finally did, George headed for home. And never came near Jocko again.

When fall arrived, I started wondering how I was going to winter Jocko, since Esther and Poogie were still adamant—and rightly so—about not sharing their house with him. One day a fellow from Marengo named Tommy Thompson stopped at the station, saw Jocko, and asked what I would take for him. I told him twelve dollars. He paid me, put Jocko in his car, and drove away.

1939

The Main Street I knew in 1914 slowly vanished.

In 1921, the Hammond brothers constructed a two-story building on the vacant lot left where fire had destroyed Alf Tillery's livery stable and Billy Cummins's restaurant back in 1913.

C. J. Sams had a garage on the lower floor, and the Masonic Lodge, which had been upstairs over the bank, moved to the second floor of this new building. The Odd Fellows, who had been upstairs in my dad's building, and the Modern Woodmen, who had used the second floor of the Boyd Building, both moved into the hall vacated by the Masons. (Most of the Odd Fellows were also Modern Woodmen.)

This was a good move on the part of the Odd Fellows, because in 1924 Patton and Hammond's drugstore, the ice cream parlor that had replaced Rile Roberson's butcher shop, and my dad's monument shop all burned. Dad saved his business records, but the fire destroyed his equipment, his tools, and even ruined all the marble and granite monuments by causing them to crack into small pieces when the cold water hit them.

The Hammond brothers bought my dad's lot and immediately rebuilt. By 1925 there was a two-story brick building with a drugstore, a restaurant, a meat market, and a bakery downstairs and a large open hall upstairs that was used for basketball and roller skating. The building had no soundproofing of any kind, and on skating nights, about twice a week, there was a steady roar in the drugstore and restaurant. Customers soon got used to the noise and just talked a little louder.

My dad took a job as manager at the basket factory for a couple of years, then rebuilt his monument business next to Sams' Garage and the Masonic Lodge. This was not a particularly good choice of location, because less than three years later, in April of 1929, the garage and Masonic Lodge burned. Dad was lucky this time; his business was saved.

Old Mr. Mason, who made canes, eventually moved in with his children. His house was torn down when the movie theater was built in 1922.

By 1928 the frame building that had housed Lambdin's law office and Blind Connor's grocery was the Crawford County Security Company and a restaurant run by Claude Brown.

I don't remember what happened to Blind Connor, but I'm sure he didn't die in English. He must have sold out and moved away—quite a decision for a successfully established blind man.

He had no family locally, so maybe he spent his last years with relatives somewhere. I hope so. Had he stayed, he would have been burned out in October of 1928, along with Brown's Barber Shop and the telephone exchange. Both of the old wooden buildings were destroyed and were replaced with one made of brick.

Joe Finch closed his saloon during Prohibition and rented the building. Cricket Sarles was operating a restaurant there when it burned in 1926.

The newspaper office and James Hankin's photography studio became Hooley Austin's shoe shop and Bloomer Bennett's radio and washing machine business. They were burned out just before Christmas in 1930.

That fire was discovered about dawn and the building was soon a smoldering ruin. When the bank opened at eight o'clock, most of the townspeople were down the street looking at the remains of Hooley's and Bloomer's businesses. Three armed men walked into the bank and robbed it of about $4000. It was rumored that the robbers had set the fire as a diversion.

Four men were implicated—one drove the getaway car—and three of them were apprehended. One of the three was a man named Welch who had at one time lived in English. He was sentenced to sixteen years at the state prison in Michigan City. He was paroled after eight years and later returned to English.

After his return, Welch occasionally hung out at the monument shop and one day in 1939 he told my brother Clyde and me how they pulled off the robbery. He had been the driver of the getaway car—which was stolen. It was a 1929 Ford Sports Roadster (at least they had good taste in cars) with a rumble seat. They parked on Fifth Street in front of Henry Mock's law office and Welch stayed in the car with the side curtains up and sitting low in the seat so he couldn't be seen and recognized.

The three other men went into the bank. The leader, a man named Bill, had a cigar box under his arm. In a few minutes, they came out with the loot in the box. Bill jumped into the front seat and the other two climbed into the rumble seat. They drove almost to French Lick on county roads, then pulled off at the edge of a field, got out and sat down on the ground. Bill opened the cigar box and dealt each stack of money around like a deck of cards. Each man got whatever he was dealt, regardless of the denomination. Welch wound up with about a thousand dollars, but Bill seemed to get much more.

They drove into French Lick and Welch left them and walked to the home of some relatives. He had visited only a few minutes when his cousin came running in with the news of the robbery. He said some were expecting the robbers to come through by way of Hall's Orchard Road and he was going to drive out to see if they would catch them. Welch said he would come along.

They found two farmers waiting at a narrow bridge. One had a .45 caliber pistol and the other had a pitchfork. They chatted a while and Welch told his cousin he didn't believe the robbers were coming that way. They wished the farmers luck and returned to French Lick.

Later, his cousin took him to Huntingburg and he caught the train to Louisville. He told us he felt very uncomfortable when the train stopped in English.

Two of the other robbers were named Sutherland and Philpot. Sutherland didn't know it, but his wife had been seeing another man—a railroad detective. When his wife told the detective about her husband's sudden prosperity, it wasn't long before Sutherland was picked up for questioning. He confessed, implicating Philpot and Welch. All any of them knew about the ringleader was that he called himself Bill. "Bill" was never caught. And, Welch claimed the fire that had diverted everybody's attention was only a coincidence.

Jim Turley's hardware store burned in the spring of 1932. Several residences were also destroyed, but the fire never spread to the business district.

Prohibition ended in 1933 and it didn't take long for the saloons to reopen. Beer was the first beverage available and the

Green Lantern Cafe in the new Hammond building was one of the first to sell it. It was crowded every night.

A major facelift for Main Street came in 1935, when new concrete streets and sidewalks were added. (That was the end of the chips made by the World War I tank.) The work took most of the summer, and when the old bridge was taken out, Ed Moore's restaurant near the depot was cut off from the main part of town. Ed put a foot log across the creek for his customers to use. He also had a beer and whiskey license, so a lot of his customers may have found getting across much easier than going home. When the new streets were finished in September, there was a big street dance.

In February 1937, English suffered a flood of semi-biblical proportions in that it rained for more than twenty days and nights. The creeks were in and out of their banks, but the real damage was to the towns along the Ohio. State Road 56 between Paoli and Salem was flooded in places, but trucks could get through. That was the only way I could get my gasoline and oil back to English.

One trip I remember particularly well. The ground was soft from all the rain and, as I backed out of the bulk plant with a full load, I cut the turn a little short, ran off the gravel drive, and the right rear wheels on my truck sank all the way down to the frame. Bud Marshall, who worked at the plant, knew a fellow who had a winch. We went to his house and his wife told us he was at the depot meeting a trainload of flood victims. We went to the depot and arrived just as the train pulled in. There were about two or three hundred refugees who had lost everything in the flood and as they stepped off the train, the good people of Salem met them and took them into their homes. Bud Marshall later did the same with a family and kept them for about two weeks. We finally found the fellow we were looking for and he managed to get me pulled out of the mud.

That summer, the bend in Camp Fork Creek just east of the

bridge was straightened. In September, Peter Gottfried died. He was the last Civil War veteran in Crawford County.

Early in 1939, plans were announced for a new "Community Building" to be constructed on North Main Street. It would have a basketball court, a stage for plays and programs, and seating for several hundred people. Everyone was asked to donate as much money, labor, and materials as possible.

Codger and I owned a ton-and-a-half Dodge flatbed truck that we agreed to make available for hauling building materials. We were told that someone would come by the next morning to pick it up. The driver turned out to be George Sloan.

We warned George that the truck was difficult to shift and that the brakes weren't very good. He listened, nodded a lot, and got behind the wheel. He drove away—and into a telephone pole. George and the pole weren't injured, but the right front of our truck was badly crumpled. The Community Building was finished without any further participation from Codger and me.

My brother Junior had graduated from high school the previous spring. Dad's health was failing, and Junior was always available to drive him wherever he needed to go. He also worked for us part-time at the station. July 22 was the Saturday night of the Reunion, and Junior left work a little early because he had a date with a girl named Edith Real. Junior had Dad's car, but he and Edith decided to go to a dance near Ferdinand with two other couples. He parked the car across from the station and dropped off the keys so Esther and I could use it if we wanted—my car wasn't running very well. That was typical of Junior. Unlike his older brothers, he didn't smoke, drink, swear, or think of himself first.

About nine o'clock, Codger, Roy, and I were about ready to close the station when the phone rang. I answered. It was Dr. Lukemeyer at Huntingburg. He asked if I was a brother to Junior Roberts. I was already thinking the worst. "He has been in an accident and is in serious condition. Come at once."

I rushed home and got Esther. Codger told Roy to wait at the station and we would call from Huntingburg. The three of us got in Codger's car and arrived in Huntingburg within the hour. Junior was still alive, but unconscious. A few minutes later, he was gone.

Apparently Junior had been thrown out when the driver lost control on a sharp curve and the car turned over. No one else was seriously injured. The State Police said no alcohol was involved.

Codger called Roy, and he went to the house and woke up Dad. About one o'clock, Dad and Clyde arrived at Dr. Lukemeyer's office. They didn't know Junior was dead and Dad was planning to have him taken to the hospital. I had to tell him the bad news. He immediately broke down and we helped him into the back room where Junior was. What a terrible, terrible night.

At the station, we always listed all of each day's paid-out items on a slip of adding machine paper, which was left in the cash register. When I arrived the next morning, there was the previous day's slip where Junior had left it, with all the items listed, including the two dollars he had taken for his pay.

Nobody stopped to think much about it at the time but, by 1939, the wooden buildings and gravel streets of 1914 had been replaced by a Main Street of brick and concrete. Wagons and teams were now as rare as automobiles had once been. Almost everybody had telephones and, for the most part, indoor plumbing. Radios and electrical appliances were commonplace. Admission to the theater went up from twenty cents to a quarter. The street lights even stayed on all night. My hometown had grown up and so had I, with a wife, a home, and a new career. But why think about the past when the future held so much promise? I didn't.

In September, Hitler invaded Poland. No one was very concerned about it—I know I wasn't. People didn't expect the United States to get involved. As soon as England and France declared war on Germany, everyone thought it would end quickly and be forgotten. After all, we had already had a World War to end all wars.

Nothing like that could ever happen again.

Epilogue

When I was a boy, we would look forward to four or five floods each year. The rain-swollen creek would overflow and all of us kids would have a great time wading and swimming in the muddy water. There was hardly ever any damage and it was seldom that the water would get into anyone's home.

We were always anxious to go to our swimming holes after a flood. Some of the deeper places would fill in with creek gravel and be knee deep, while the shallow places would wash out and be over our heads. At least there was always a good place to swim.

One of the reasons that the basket factory came to English in 1921 was the abundant supply of virgin beech trees that covered the neighboring hills. As the beech trees and other virgin timber disappeared, so did the protection they offered from the summer rains, which could now drain more easily and quickly into the creeks.

And the floods began to get worse.

The first of the really damaging floods came in 1937. English wasn't the hardest hit, but there was water in all the businesses on Main Street and in most of the homes in the west end.

In January of 1959, it warmed up enough one day to rain instead of snow. It didn't rain a lot, but the ground was

Main Street Flooded (looking north) About 1910
Photo by James E. Hankins.

frozen and none of the water could soak into the soil. There was about three feet of water in the stores on Main Street and only slightly less in my bulk plant. And then the temperature dropped back to normal—or below. Everything that was wet immediately froze. That was really a mess. I had to borrow a motor for my pump before I could take care of my customers.

On June 9, 1979, the rains came and the water was a foot deep in most of the businesses on Main Street. After a few days of throwing away carpeting and cleaning off muddy walls, life was back to normal. For about six weeks.

July 26, 1979 was the beginning of the end for Main Street. In a few frightening hours the water rose to ceiling-level in the business district. Almost everyone had harrowing tales of narrow escapes and heroic efforts. Miraculously, there was no loss of life. But there was much damage. Most of the homes in the west end, where Three Forks of Little Blue began, were destroyed. Homeowners in a floodplain are, by law, not allowed to rebuild there, and soon the bulldozers arrived and did their sad work. For the first time since 1814, Moses Smith's property was once again grass and trees.

Hartford—and Main Street—would be next.

About three o'clock in the morning on June 7, 1990, the flood waters began rising again. The sheriff's department, the town marshal, and the fire department started knocking on doors, warning people to evacuate. By dawn, the flood peaked at about half the 1979 level. Enough was enough. Businesspeople and homeowners applied to the Federal Emergency Management Agency (FEMA) for assistance to move the town out of the floodplain.

As of this writing, English, Indiana is planning to relocate to higher, dryer, ground. The new west end will include the old Reunion grounds where the Civil War veterans camped out and ate their beans and potatoes. Toney Cave will be in the middle of a residential area—and will probably be filled in. James Sloan's cabin was always at the outskirts of town, and would have continued to be if it, too, hadn't been dismantled and moved away.

And Main Street? Well, whatever they rename Highway 64 between the new city limits, and regardless of how swiftly and completely the bulldozers descend, Main Street will still be where it always has been, etched simultaneously in gravel and wood, concrete and brick, and populated with a lifetime of familiar faces and names. And always, always echoing with the excitement of a Saturday night crowd.

I wouldn't have it any other way.

E. C. Roberts (1989)